FITZCARRALDO

LUTZ KOEPNICK

CAMDEN HOUSE

First published 2019 by Camden House

Camden House is an imprint of Boydell & Brewer Inc.
668 Mt. Hope Avenue, Rochester, NY 14620, USA
www.camden-house.com
and of Boydell & Brewer Limited
PO Box 9, Woodbridge, Suffolk IP12 3DF, UK
www.boydellandbrewer.com

ISBN-13: 978-1-64014-036-3
ISBN-10: 1-64014-036-0

Library of Congress Cataloging-in-Publication Data

Names: Koepnick, Lutz P. (Lutz Peter), author.
Title: Fitzcarraldo / Lutz Koepnick.
Description: Rochester, New York : Camden House, [2019] | Series: Camden
    House German film classics | Includes bibliographical references.
Identifiers: LCCN 2019020771| ISBN 9781640140363 (pbk. : alk. paper) | ISBN
    1640140360 (pbk. : alk. paper)
Subjects: LCSH: Fitzcarraldo (Motion picture)
Classification: LCC PN1997.2.F58 K63 2019 | DDC 791.43/72—dc23 LC
    record available at https://lccn.loc.gov/2019020771

This publication is printed on acid-free paper.
Printed in the United States of America.

Fitzcarraldo

Spectacle in the Forest

His arms are stretched wide, his eyes face vast areas of land in front of his body, the camera—located behind his back—invites the viewer to see what he sees. Actors assume such postures when reaping their audience's applause after the end of a show. Soccer stars are known for such gestures so as to marshal their fans' gratitude after shooting a memorable goal. Dictators have been seen standing like this on elevated platforms eager to enthuse themselves by rousing a crowd's emotions. But the man we see, and whose seeing we are seeing, is

"I am the spectacle in the forest."

neither an artist nor an athlete nor a politician. Our times might call him a venture capitalist, might even celebrate him as a fearless entrepreneur of first rank. His own times, the years around 1900, have no real concept, no place for him except at the fringes of the known world, of the ordinary and the accepted.

In spite of its wrinkles and stains, his white linen suit—so much is clear—causes him to stand out amid his fellow travelers. He is no doubt a man of resolve and boundless energy, a man whose uncompromising visions claim the same extreme effort from others that he demands from himself. Minutes earlier we heard someone call him a conqueror of the useless, but similar to how Romantic geniuses were believed to create the very norms meant to assess their achievements, so this man in white does not hesitate to recast failure as success and find exhilarating value in what common sense considers vain, void of utility, bizarre, a mere figment of the imagination, sheer madness. Calculating divisions of means and ends cannot but appear nonsensical to him, not least of all because in his view visionary actions carry their meaning in themselves and will always exceed the value others ascribe to goal-oriented activities upfront. Nietzsche, who descended into mental illness a few years prior to this man's ecstatic facing of the world, would have recognized him as a kindred spirit: a bold maker of new worlds emancipated from the maps of good and evil. The captains of our own neoliberal present might reclaim him as an icon of successful self-management and ruthless risk-taking: a man endorsing the fact that every man fights for himself and—because social contracts, bonds, and obligations are presumed to be the shackles of bureaucratic states and governments—has learned how to trust in nothing but his own will, his ambition to move mountains when necessary. For him, there is no real difference between words and actions, stories and deeds. His doing generates its own narratives. He shows to tell, tells to show, whether or not possible audiences understand his gestures and metaphors of thought and action. He eagerly proclaims to embody a spectacle in the forest even if only trees, birds, and pigs serve as primary witnesses to his endeavors. Foolish struggles fill this man's heart. We are meant to imagine him as happy.

And yet, in spite of his insularity, countless stories have been told about this man in white, Brian Sweeney Fitzgerald, about the actor presenting his pursuits in front of the camera, Klaus Kinski, and about the director Werner Herzog mobilizing unprecedented resources to project his Amazonian venture onto screens. In fact, numerous tales and legends about *Fitzcarraldo*—its precarious production history in Peru between 1977 and 1981, the strained relationship between actor and filmmaker, the director's unyielding use of indigenous people and lands during the film's making—met possible audiences long before the film premiered in West-German cinemas in March 1982 and moved on to win Herzog best director at the Cannes film festival that same year, among other distinctions. Les Blank's *Burden of Dreams* (1982), chronicling various episodes in *Fitzcarraldo*'s making, mostly between April and June 1981, had already been screened as a forty-minute work in progress at the Telluride Film Festival in September 1981. German audiences, on the other hand, had read about the project in various magazine articles as early as in the late 1970s. Some of these reports exposed alleged human rights violations, others detailed Herzog's desire to haul a 320-ton steamship over a small mountain in the jungle as a project no less crazed and neo-colonial than Fitzcarraldo's hope to bring European opera to the Amazon.

Troubling tales and legends, including those emanating from Herzog's many pronouncements about this film, preceded the opening of the film and have come to guide its reception over the last four decades, so much so that most viewers will find it difficult to approach *Fitzcarraldo* on its own terms, let alone not to attend to its images, sounds, performances, and narrative as media irreducibly blurring the lines between fiction and reality, between character, actor, and director. It seems as if everyone has always known, and continues to know, what *Fitzcarraldo* is all about long before the film's first image of a mountainous jungle landscapes draped in fog—an image actually borrowed from Blank's documentary footage and hence blown up from 16 to 35 millimeters—fills the screen. *Fitzcarraldo*, we have been told and learned to accept, is all about Herzog, is all about Kinski. It is about one substituting for the other. No matter its historical setting and fictional momentum, the film, according to whatever you hear, see, and read about *Fitzcarraldo*, is all about two legendary best f(r)iends navigating at the edge of reason to transform the world into an uncompromising work of art, an operatic spectacle that denies physical suffering and exploits humans and natural environments to showcase the power of individual willfulness.

There is little doubt that *Fitzcarraldo*'s production history is extraordinary indeed. The film vastly exceeded its budget in both financial and temporal terms. Early filming was disrupted by unforeseen political hostilities in Northern Peru as well as conflicts with the Aguaruna communities, who refused to serve as mere props in dramas staged by outsiders and requested payments for their collaboration that did not simply take their underprivileged position in Peruvian society for granted. German activists distributed photographs of Nazi concentration camps to tribal members to intimate the direction of Herzog's project. Death threats were made. One of the crew's camps in the jungle was surrounded by armed Indians and burned down, causing crew members to flee the premises with their canoes and wave white flags in gestures of surrender. It took Herzog a year to relocate the production about fifteen hundred miles to the south, identify new locales for shooting key sequences, and broker a deal with local Machiguenga Indians to support the film's production and provide extras for the filming. The problems, however, were by no means over. Various tribal conflicts resulted in arrows being shot at crew members. Both steamships hauled into the jungle to film Fitzcarraldo's foray into rubber extraction got stuck for weeks on end due to historically low water levels. The engineer hired to pull one of the two ships across a steep section of land between the Rio Camisea and the Rio Urubamba quit the production, not just frustrated by Herzog's and executive producer Walter Saxer's demands, but no longer able to guarantee the safety of all those involved in the filming. Small planes hired to transport crew members and material to remote locations crashed in difficult flying conditions. Equipment shipments were rerouted and delayed, including the delivery of a Caterpillar D-8 bulldozer from Miami, whose role in clearing a path through the trees and dragging the ship up and down a 40-degree slope was critical. Various Machiguengas lost their lives in proximity to the filming process, not as a direct result of the production efforts as some commentators initially wanted to have it, but nevertheless casting troubling shadows over the work of the production unit as whole.

Once you add to all this the casting challenges the project met throughout the entire production process, much of what was reported about *Fitzcarraldo*'s folly circa 1981 certainly seemed to hit the mark. Due to Herzog's refusal to rely on elaborate special effects and his insistence on the authenticity of location work, initial talks with major Hollywood studios to finance the film and have Jack Nicholson play its protagonist collapsed early on. Warren Oates was under discussion for the title role in late 1979, yet was never officially contracted, only to then be replaced by Jason Robards, with Mick Jagger being recruited for the role of Fitzcarraldo's somewhat dim-witted sidekick Wilbur. During the first phase of the actual shooting in early 1981, after about forty percent of the film's footage had already been secured, Robards contracted amoebic dysentery and had to return to the US for medical treatment; much to Herzog's dismay, Robards's doctors and lawyers ordered the actor not to return to the film set because of its unhealthy general conditions. With Robards gone and the need not only to find another actor but to reshoot a whole number of scenes, Jagger had to withdraw from the project as well in order to ready himself for a new tour, a loss that Herzog considered one of the most painful of his career as director and that caused him to eliminate the role of Wilbur altogether. In the face of seeing the whole production collapse, Herzog in late February 1981 first considered taking on the role of his protagonist himself— "Why," Herzog asked in his diary on February 18, 1981, "should I not play Fitzcarraldo myself? I would trust myself to do it because my project and the character have become identical"[1]—before he then moved on to draft the impulsive German actor Klaus Kinski for the role, with whom Herzog had already worked in *Aguirre, The Wrath of God* (1972), *Nosferatu* (1979), and *Woyzeck* (1979).

In retrospect, even when reviewing early footage with Robards and Jagger, it has become impossible to think of *Fitzcarraldo* without Kinski's iconic presence. And yet, once Kinski arrived in Peru in April 1981 and filming resumed, the actor's notorious temper tantrums, his mental instability, his idiosyncrasies, and his volatile behavior toward other actors, crew members, producers, and directors—all this certainly added additional trials to the project and pushed it, almost daily, to the brink of disaster. Amid the filming's turmoil in both the Amazon jungle and the river town Iquitos in northeastern Peru, Italian actress Claudia Cardinale provided the perhaps most balanced and levelheaded element. Set to play Fitzcarraldo's girlfriend Molly, the owner of a successful bordello in Iquitos, her kindness and professionalism at times even managed to calm Kinski's demons and allowed for the principal shooting to conclude in mid-July 1981. Though the film pushed up against and exceeded various budget plans during its lengthy production phase, it is reported that in the end Herzog's 158-minute film needed a total of 14 million Deutschmark—the historical equivalent of about $7 million—in order to be completed, a fraction of, for instance, the $31.5 million it took Francis Ford Coppola to film, during the same period, another descent into a jungle's heart of darkness in *Apocalypse Now* (1979).

After editing most of the character-centered footage in late summer and early fall in West Germany, Herzog returned to the

Early production footage with Jason Robards and Mick Jagger, in *Burden of Dreams* (1982, dir. Les Blank); *New York Times* clipping.

Peruvian jungle once more in October 1981 to capture on film what had promised, in the minds of both the film's director and his protagonist, the project's most triumphant moment: the ship's successful crossing of the mountain. In early November, with all principal filming finally coming to a conclusion, Herzog noted in his journal: "There was no pain, no joy, no excitement, no relief, no happiness, no sound, not even a deep breath. All I grasped was a profound uselessness, or to be more precise, I had merely penetrated deeper into its mysterious realm. I saw the ship, returned to its element, right itself with a weary sigh. Today, on Wednesday, the 4th of November 1981, shortly after twelve noon, we got the ship from the Rio Camisea over a mountain into the Rio Urubamba. All that is to be reported is this: I took part."[2] The aloofness of Herzog's entry might puzzle at first. That Herzog after years of strenuous labor situates himself as a mere witness, a distant observer, is as bewildering as his effort to endow the ship, the *Molly Aida*, with a certain form of agency. Recording the sigh of the ship, Herzog's note makes it sound as if it had been pulled across the land against its own will and could now finally resume its suspended life: as if its ultimate return to the river evidenced nothing but the material world's often invisible, albeit obstinate vibrancy; as if humans therefore even in moments of perceived triumph could not but fail to ever assume full control over the world around them.

Readers familiar with the long history of Herzog's self-commentary will recognize in his statement of November 1981 certain echoes of his persistent toying with ideas of the sublime, his hovering between stances of human grandiosity and humbleness. They will not hesitate to see it as yet another instance of the director's at times bombastic, at times ironic gestures to infuse our modern world of machines, technologies, media, and rationality with quasi-Romantic sensibilities, not simply in order to find magic and wonder where others have long resorted to cynical disenchantment, but also to present his own directorial activity as something that exceeds pedestrian justification, explanation, and historicization, as a force sui generis. Herzog's fatigued coolness at the banks of the Rio Urubamba, in this view, simply served as yet another strategy to express the very megalomania that at some point during the project had caused the director to believe he could and should take on the role of his protagonist himself.

But wait. Perhaps we can also take a cue from Herzog's final restraint simply to ask what the film itself tells, shows, and knows independent of its own maker's vision and intention, his rationalizations and self-commentaries, his fables about the production as much as all the different legends that seem to preempt any viewing of *Fitzcarraldo* today. No matter the extent to which it may simply represent yet another strategy of performance, Herzog's detachment at the end of the filming recognizes the possibility that objects, including the objects we associate with art and filmmaking, might assume a life, power, and vibrancy of their own. It urges us to think of the world of objects not as numb, dumb, and passive matter that requires strong authorial efforts to acquire meaning; but as something that has protean forms of agency and therefore does not pivot around human intentionality. By letting us hearing the ship sigh, Herzog—perhaps contrary to his own intention—calls on us to read the film against the grain of what we (and he) are eager, willing, accustomed, or predisposed to read into it. He invites us to brush aside his own willfulness when making the film, to look beyond his signatures embedded in the final product, to explore how *Fitzcarraldo*'s images and sounds themselves might rub against the diegetic and extra-diegetic legends, wills, and intentions that we have come to associate with the film's protagonist and maker. What Herzog in this moment of contemplative detachment encourages future viewers to do is to attend to nothing less than his film's own sighs, that is, to register moments when *Fitzcarraldo* seems to assume a life of its own and exceeds, contains, undermines, suspends, or emancipates itself from what its filmmaker and diegetic hero sought to accomplish in the Peruvian jungle.

Men and their boats: Kinski in *Fitzcarraldo*, Herzog in *Burden of Dreams.*

Think of the image showing Kinski in the role of Fitzcarraldo above the treetops, his arms and eyes stretched wide, as such a moment of cinematic sighing. The scene actually starts with the sight of four men—Fitzcarraldo, the steamship's Captain (Paul Hittscher), its cook Huerequeque (Huerequeque Enrique Bohorquez), and its mechanic Cholo (Miguel Ángel Fuentes)—standing together on a makeshift platform in a tree, it being unclear how they got up there in the first place, as no ladder or other climbing device is visible. The camera, in a vertiginous aerial movement, circles for more than 360 degrees around this platform, eventually allowing the bodies of all four men to drop below the frame. We then cut to a two-shot of captain and mechanic before the camera veers to the left to capture Fitzcarraldo, his finger first pointing at the Rio Ucayali (as it is named in the film) on the left, and then with grand gestures taking hold over the camera's movement to direct his companions' as much as our attention to the Rio Pachitea (as it is named in the film) on his right and to reveal his plan to haul the steamship across the territory between the two rivers. Some dialogue with restless camera movements ensues between the men on the platform before the camera finally positions itself behind the body of Kinski and frames him in the imperial posture described earlier.

The whole series of shots takes less than a minute. And yet, what we come to witness is not only a volatile drama between Fitzcarraldo and his crew, but also a precarious conflict between Fitzcarraldo's efforts to define the visual field, his effort to translate inner visions into domineering optical perspectives, on the one hand, and on the other the camera's ability to capture the protagonist's politics of vision. Due to considerable space restrictions on the platform, Thomas Mauch's camera never assumes the optical confidence Fitzcarraldo's uncompromising leadership claims for itself. The disquiet of the frame cannot but articulate the feverish recklessness of Fitzcarraldo's revelation. Moreover, any viewer familiar with Herzog's *Aguirre, the Wrath of God*, when initially witnessing the

Heroic vision?

camera's dizzying move around the platform, will no doubt recall the final shot of Herzog's earlier Amazon epic: Herzog's prolonged circling around the rebel's raft that collapsed Aguirre's vision of progress back into the mythic standstill of circular time and precisely thus unraveled the very visual regime the film's protagonist sought to impose on his contemporaries and on us as his viewers. As majestic as the spin around the platform in the trees in *Fitzcarraldo* at first sight might appear, it at the same time has the power to disassociate us from Fitzcarraldo's heroic vision and, by containing his zeal for progressive temporality within the physicality of circular movement, communicate its folly. What the scene stages is a profound tension between the metaphorical and the material, the visionary and the technological, between Fitzcarraldo's celebration of control and agency and the camera's own agential powers, its sighing refusal to submit to what Fitzcarraldo wants it to do.

Shot toward the very end of the period film historians have come to identify as the heyday of New German Cinema, *Fitzcarraldo* is a film with precarious beginnings and unsettled endings. Thick mythologies generated by the film's makers as much as its critics have made it difficult to watch the film itself doing its work, that is, to recognize the extent to which *Fitzcarraldo's* vibrant sounds and images push up against or sigh about the film's narrative, its hero's performative presence, its director's authorial signatures. *Fitzcarraldo* is about much more than featuring imperial madness and celebrating conquests of the useless. It is about the limits of human agency, meaning-making, and happiness. It is about how modern concepts of individual authorship and control over nature have generated the opposite, namely a situation in which our presumed power to change the course of the Earth has created unprecedented forms of dependency and increasingly calls into question what it might mean to be human in the first place. At heart, *Fitzcarraldo* is therefore also about how we should attend to the objects we call films, about the relationship between the human and animated matter, and it is to these questions that the following pages will repeatedly return.

Dreams (That Money Can't Buy)

Fitzcarraldo's tells a story that unsettles the boundaries between dream and reality. Dreams and dreamlike visions cause the film's protagonist to pursue a rather reckless expedition and engineering venture, but the longer we follow our hero's travails, the more reality itself takes on the dimension of a dream and the less we seem to know whose dreaming we are actually witnessing. Fitzcarraldo's dream is as simple as it is outrageous: to stage grand European opera and bring legendary tenor Enrico Caruso, whose performance in Verdi's *Ernani* Fitzcarraldo witnesses in Manaus in the film's elaborate opening sequence, to the Amazonian port town of Iquitos. Once back in Iquitos, Fitzcarraldo, with the help of his girlfriend Molly, seeks to find possible sponsors for his project among the town's decadently wealthy rubber barons. But to no avail. Fitzcarraldo is well known for grandiose, albeit unfinished, perhaps even unfinishable projects: his Trans-Andean railway construction got stuck in the thicket of the jungle after a few hundred yards; his idea to produce ice was too much ahead of its time and lacked proper capitalization. It therefore comes as no surprise that the town's financial elite prefers to feed their money to the fish rather than invest it in the building of a stately opera house, to ridicule the European as an unhinged outcast rather than to embrace high art as a medium to legitimize or showcase their own financial snobbery.

But for all his eccentricity and capriciousness, Fitzcarraldo is not a man to give up easily. In fact, the more the real seems to turn against him, the more he allows visions and dreams to drive his being in the world. With Molly's support he acquires a piece of land to extract rubber from its trees and thus generate the capital necessary for his cultural mission. The double catch: Peruvian law requires that purchased land be taken physically into possession within nine months, and the territory in question makes any successful exploitation of natural resources seemingly impossible because unpassable rapids separate it from any existing trade route. Fitzcarraldo's idea to solve the problem is as ingenious as it is crazy. Having studied the region's map extensively, he knows that a passable river—the Rio Pachitea—is close to the unpassable river—the Rio Ucayali—a few miles upstream from the rapids. His plan, therefore, is to acquire a steamship, travel up the Pachitea, haul the ship across the land to the Ucayali, and then use the ship as a shuttle between the crossing and the area of extraction while transporting the rubber with another ship on the Pachitea back to Iquitos. Aside from the challenge of moving a steamship from one river bed to another, there is one more catch: a few years prior, a group of missionaries traveling up the Pachitea had fallen prey to a tribe of Indians who resisted geographical intrusion and spiritual colonization. Not much is known about the actual fate of these missionaries. What is known, however, is the fact that any travels up the Pachitea are ill advised.

While his crew remains mostly in the dark about Fitzcarraldo's scheme, the *Molly Aida* takes off from Iquitos toward the Pachitea. Its first stop is the overgrown Trans-Andean railway station to pick up a few railway tracks, its second—some way up the river already—the missionary station of Samamiriza, where our protagonist hopes to learn more about the disaster of the missionaries' expedition of 1896. Once we find the steamship en route again, the narrative's pace decelerates dramatically and we enter the dreamlike. Ominous drumming reaches the *Molly Aida*, which Fitzcarraldo tries to silence by playing a Caruso record. An umbrella floats down the river, interpreted by our travelers as a sign of warning. We repeatedly witness Fitzcarraldo and his men staring at the passing trees without being able to detect anything; the threats of deadly encounters play out mostly along the audible, not the visible. Some crew members

The christening of the *Molly Aida*.

flee the ship in terror and head back to Iquitos. Others get so drunk that they do not notice when a multitude of Indians enter the scene after all, first blocking any possible return passage, then appearing more friendly, even collaborative, because they seem to mistake the ship and its white-clothed entrepreneur for embodiments of an ancient prophecy.

Eventually, the *Molly Aida* arrives at the site that Fitzcarraldo, by studying the map, has identified as the area of terrestrial passage. Time fizzles, becomes fuzzy. Undertaken with the help of the members of the local Jívaros tribe, hauling the steamship to the Ucayali takes many weeks and months of plot time, but days and weeks seem to bleed into one another and escape the measurable. What took Herzog himself months and years to plan and execute, in the end occupies about thirty-five minutes of screen time. Once the ship is back in the water, dreams transform into nightmares. Because, as it will turn out, the Jívaros had a very different understanding of Fitzcarraldo's mission than our protagonist himself does, they cut the *Molly Aida* loose overnight, allow it to float down the Ucayali through the Pongo das Mortes, the very rapids Fitzcarraldo's elaborate scheme had sought to circumvent, and thus annul the entire project. Drunk from the previous night's festivities, Fitzcarraldo and his men wake up too late, and too much in a daze, to reverse the ship's course. All that is left is to return home empty handed.

Not entirely, though. On its sad way back, the badly damaged *Molly Aida* docks at the prosperous rubber plantation of Don Auqilino (José Lewgoy), who not only buys the steamship from the bankrupt Fitzcarraldo, but informs him about a touring opera company in Manaus and permits Fitzcarraldo to use the *Molly Aida* for two more weeks to journey home to Iquitos. Though we do not learn exactly what kind of deal Fitzcarraldo brokered with the company, in the film's last sequence we witness singers, musicians, and props boarding the *Molly Aida* and sailing up the Amazon back to Iquitos. The final shots alternate between images of the company performing Bellini's *I Puritani* (1834) on board; of Molly and the people of Iquitos cheering the return of the ship, bedazzled about the fact that it returned from the opposite direction; and, perhaps most importantly, of Fitzcarraldo, a large cigar in his mouth, a giant red director's chair placed behind him, his face full of joy and triumph about the fact that he—the conqueror of the useless—has brought

The return of the *Molly Aida*.

the pleasures of European high art to the jungle town of Iquitos after all.

The stories that have attached themselves to *Fitzcarraldo* before and after the film's making, the myths and metaphors that internally drive and comment on the film's actions, Herzog's own incessant efforts over the years to frame any possible viewing of the film— all this tends to obscure rather than sharpen our attention for the film's narrative elements and structure. Powerful images, in Herzog's work, often seem to suspend questions about narrative coherence and plausibility; the affects produced by exalted diegetic or non-diegetic sounds displace conventional expectations about effective story constructions. Narratological approaches to *Fitzcarraldo* may thus resemble archeological efforts: one needs to dig through various strata of sedimented material to lay one's finger on how the film organizes its plot, how it arranges and paces narrative time for the viewer. But even though distributors and streaming services today often categorize *Fitzcarraldo* generically as an adventure film, no one—one might respond—watches Herzog to consume and be consumed by well-told stories. Narrative, in Herzog, is instead a mere hook, a vehicle, to explore the power of inner visions, a particular character's mindscapes, the ecstasies potent sounds and images elicit. To subject any of his films to narrative analysis is therefore to muddy the extent to which the logic of dreams, the dreamlike, grafts itself onto what Herzog's protagonists experience as the exigencies of the real and its structures of temporality. Stories in Herzog's oeuvre are the mere veil through which his audiences are meant to behold of the generative energy of visions, the power of dreams to build rather than merely respond to the world.

It should therefore come as no surprise that the oneiric and hallucinatory take center stage in *Fitzcarraldo* as well and overshadow the work of the film's narrative. When Fitzcarraldo visits the missionary station, the following dialogue ensues between an elderly missionary and our protagonist about the obstinacy of dreams and the resulting difficulties of converting the Indians to Catholicism:

> Jesuit Missionary: "We can't cure them of the idea that our normal life is only an illusion behind which lies the reality of dreams."
> Fitzcarraldo: "This interests me very much. You know, I am a man of the opera."

The leap in Fitzcarraldo's response, collapsing the world of dreams with the highly stylized realm of operatic performance, is at first perhaps as puzzling as the Jesuits' efforts to challenge conceptions of human existence that separate material from spiritual dimensions, the noumenal from the phenomenological. The Indians' dualism, in the eyes of the Jesuit, seems to threaten the paths of Christianization. It devalues the grasp of religious dogmas and worldly codes of conduct and thus creates zones of unacceptable ambiguity. For Fitzcarraldo, on the other hand, the art of opera taps into and is energized precisely by what exceeds the visible. It is literally metaphysical, intensifies ordinary life, and charges the everyday with the very kind of meaning and vibrancy established codes of conduct fail to produce. What both the missionary and the aspiring entrepreneur, in spite of profound differences, agree upon is to think of dreams not as Freudian ciphers of repressed desires and distorted wish fantasies but as alternate realities, as engines of world building. Dreams, for both interlocutors, do not communicate or mirror anything as such. They have no message, no language, no code that can be read, no enigma we can decipher. They instead are the enigma we call life. Dreams in *Fitzcarraldo* are a way of knowing things, of sensing and connecting to the world, of extending mind and senses beyond routinized and disambiguated perceptions of the real. They situate and embed subjects in spaces and times that displace the categories associated with the ordinary. They in fact provide the grounds from which to create alternate architectures of life in the first place.

Missionaries among each other: "I am a man of the opera."

Throughout his career Herzog has eagerly professed to be a dreamless sleeper. But neither sleep nor rest are things viewers ever expect from Herzog or any of his protagonists. Herzog's heroes and anti-heroes are men always on the move, men driven to pursue their visions at almost all costs and in defiance of common algorithms calculating the relation of means and ends. To rest and sleep, even to dream in any conventional sense, is to surrender to the mandates of rubber barons and Jesuits, of Hollywood film studios and academic movie critics. For Herzog, as much as for Fitzcarraldo, to dream is instead to draw on the power of aesthetic experience, on intensities that exceed or defy calculation. The function of dreams is to unsettle the kind of narratives we have come to accept about the order of the day. Dreams in Herzog generate the unexpected, that which restores our ability to respond to our surroundings with awe and wonder. They are modes of being unconditionally and ecstatically awake.

"Ecstasy," derived from the ancient Greek ekstasis (ἔκστασις), means to be outside oneself, to stand on ground other than the one we call the everyday. To be ek-static is to take a stand loaded with possibility, with transformative energy that continually redraws given boundaries between subject and object, individual and world. Fitzcarraldo envisions the world as one in which sleepless ecstasy may reign triumphant, a permanent state of exception. He is always "on," yet always at the edge of or outside himself, decentered, in violation of the closures Western humanism has defined as the borders of the subject. In so doing, Fitzcarraldo makes us think about our own historical moment of 24/7 connectivity and digital distractions in which sleep, more than a century after Fitzcarraldo, becomes ever less affordable if we are to meet the expectations of self-management and self-optimization. Similar to the ecstatic entrepreneur in the jungle, our own neoliberal order of things calls upon us not simply to be always "on," but to be ever-eager to disrupt the fabric of the ordinary, to never rely on the alleged burdens of "society" or any historical networks of trust and solidarity. Unlike the world of Fitzcarraldo, however, our own era of distracted ecstasy rarely seems to grant anything we might be willing to call aesthetic and free of instrumental reason. Ours is an era in which being outside of ourselves typically means allowing other powers to rule over us; it in spite of all its stress on disruptive zealousness has little patience for dreamers, for the generative power of dreaming and the wondrous in Herzog's sense at all.

Beyond Nature and Culture

During his brief sojourn at the missionary station, Fitzcarraldo vaguely and somewhat enigmatically calls his project in the jungle "geographical" in nature. A man of maps, as viewers of the film already know by now, he wants to be seen as an explorer describing the earth in new ways. Geographers, in Fitzcarraldo's understanding, do not simply map how humans relate to their locations, regions, and environments, they actively produce these relationships. They write and rewrite the Earth. They re-engineer nature. As he hauls his steamship over the mountain, he will be doing far more than just altering the contour lines professional cartographers use to indicate different elevations, peaks, valleys, and the gradient of slopes. Fitzcarraldo's geographical project directly draws on and in so doing redraws the land. He will boldly sketch a line through the trees and the mud just as draftsmen imprint strokes on paper.

Fitzcarraldo's dedication to applied geography recalls the futile efforts of Herzog's Spanish conquistadors a decade earlier in *Aguirre, the Wrath of God*. In the previous film, European men in the Amazonian jungle draft and read stately documents with great serenity, rather ironically confusing symbolic acts of representation with acts of physical power and control. The more fragile their actual range of agency, the more imperial the tone of their documents claiming land and authority; the smaller the actual reach of their movements on the film's raft as it floats down the Amazon river, the grander their delusion of ruling the Earth and—in Aguirre's own words—of making history "as others put plays on stage."

Fitzcarraldo continues and simultaneously reverses this path. Written documents and maps are central to his journey down the

Imperial documents in *Aguirre, the Wrath of God* (1972).

river. Think of the scene in which Fitzcarraldo, at Don Auqilino's estate, lays his eyes for the first time on the (fictitious) map that graphs vacant rubber harvesting lots and shows the bends of the Ucayali and the Pachitea. Though images of ubiquitous dangers are printed on the map and warn possible travelers not to enter some of the territories depicted, the drawing instantly activates his imagination and triggers his plan of traversing the mountain, as if possible differences between two-dimensional representations and the actual features of the land were of no concern. Think of the scene in which Fitzcarraldo, right before stretching his arms wide on a platform in the trees to claim a hold over his property, fiddles with a map of unwieldy proportions in order to verify, much to the consternation of his crew, the exact location for the planned crossing.

Fitzcarraldo's maps.

Similar to the ruminations in Jorge Luis Borges's famous short story, "On Exactitude in Science," Fitzcarraldo here treats his map as if cartographic representations offered iconic doubles of the land on the same scale as the land itself: something that does not need to be read, decoded, or analyzed, because it provides a fully rendered physical stand-in for the territory in question. Think of a subsequent scene in which Fitzcarraldo illustrates his geographical project to the ship's captain: so vigorously does his hand draft lines on a blank piece of paper that the emerging map bulges and crumples, that is, presents a three-dimensional analogue to, rather than a flat representation of, the land between the rivers. Though maps play as important a role in *Fitzcarraldo* as do written documents in the colonial conquest of *Aguirre*, in the end their functions and meanings are quite different in nature. In the earlier film, marks on paper showcase the factual delusion of Herzog's protagonists, their entrapment in an ever-growing gulf between the real and their imperial fantasies. In the latter film, they embody physical action in and on the world with other means. They anticipate and extend, iconically register and energize the material marks and footprints Herzog's wild-eyed protagonist is about to imprint onto the land.

It has become commonplace to think of Fitzcarraldo's understanding of geography as a Nietzschean or Wagnerian effort to approach the world as—or transform it into—a total work of art. Fitzcarraldo treats the land like sculptors mold clay and painters cover their canvasses with potent brushstrokes. Though initially meant to be a mere step in the effort to bring grand opera to the jungle, Fitzcarraldo's geographical project, in this understanding, underwrites an uncompromising aestheticization of the world. It knows of no obligations to the land and its inhabitants other than the ones driven by aesthetic sensibilities, by the will to shape and reshape terrestrial formations, to lend form to meaningless matter, analogous to how artistic geniuses are believed to create works, forms, and artifacts from scratch. In inviting men to carve their vision into numb and dumb nature, Fitzcarraldo's geography claims that humanity's central mission is to project itself onto and precisely thus find its own mirror image in nature, to transform the messy and formless into compelling man-made artifice. Art, here, far from simply capturing the world, produces it as a playing field of human action.

Aestheticizing views of nature and the man-made world abound in Herzog's work throughout his entire career. His landscapes are landscapes of the mind as much as they describe physical realities; they are charged with expressive energies and trigger affective responses; they mimic the composition of famous paintings or serve as stages of at times heroic, at times mindless self-inquiry. Nature as such does not exist in Herzog. Like the proverbial sounds emanating from trees falling in the woods, Herzog's nature requires human perception, recording, inscription, and affect—it requires culture—to become nature in the first place. And yet, it would be foolish to equate Herzog's own position with Fitzcarraldo's. The troubled making of *Fitzcarraldo*, in fact, caused Herzog himself, in a by-now famous rant recorded in front of Les Blank's camera in June 1981, to contemplate a view of the natural world fundamentally hostile or—perhaps even worse—indifferent to human intervention:

> Of course, we are challenging nature itself. And it hits back, that's all. And that's what is grandiose about it. And we have to accept that it is much stronger than we are. Kinski always says it is full of erotic elements. I don't see it so much erotic. I see it more full of obscenity. It's just . . . . and nature here is vile and base. I wouldn't see anything erotical here. I would see fornication and asphyxiation and choking and fighting for survival and growing and just rotting away. Of course, there's a lot of misery. But it is the same misery that is all around us. The trees here are in misery and the birds are in misery. I don't think they sing. They just screech in pain.

It's an unfinished country. It's still prehistorical. The only thing that is lacking is the dinosaurs here. It's like a curse weighing on an entire landscape, and whoever goes too deep into this has his share of this curse. So we are cursed with what we are doing here. It's a land that God, if he exists, has created in anger. It's the only land where . . . where creation is unfinished yet.

Taking a close look at what's around us, there is some kind of harmony. It's the harmony of overwhelming and collective murder. And we in comparison to the articulate vileness and baseness and obscenity of all this jungle . . . we in comparison to that enormous articulation, we only sound and look like badly pronounced and half-finished sentences out of a stupid suburban novel, a cheap novel.

We have to become humble in front of this overwhelming misery and overwhelming fornication, overwhelming growth and overwhelming lack of order. Even the stars up here in the sky look like a mess. There is no harmony in the universe. We have to get acquainted to this idea that there is no real harmony as we have conceived it. But when I say this, I say this all full of admiration for the jungle. It is not that I hate it. I love it. I love it very much. But I love it against my better judgment.

Contrary to Fitzcarraldo's entrepreneurial understanding of geography, there is nothing triumphant in Herzog's vision of nature—except the triumphalist tone of shrewd wording and self-denial. His is a negative theology, a vision of nature as a horror and freak show, unresponsive to or even inimical to anything we may want to consider culture. In this rather apocalyptic conception, art and culture emerge in revolt against the crudeness of nature—not as mediums to control, shape, and utilize the non-human as Fitzcarraldo wants to have it, but as mechanisms to construct alternate worlds, however fragile and ephemeral they may be. Deeply fatigued by the process of casting Fitzcarraldo's geographical project into compelling images,

"There is no harmony in the universe" (*Burden of Dreams*).

Herzog here—unlike his protagonist—resorts to the philosophical tradition of the sublime. Nature might be overwhelming and hostile, it might resist understanding and empathy, it might repel and take revenge on any effort to control it. But in all of this the natural world not only reminds humans of their fragility and powerlessness, but invites us to recognize our own smallness as the very ground and center of what it might mean to be human in the first place.

For Herzog, Fitzcarraldo's geographical project—the construction of a terrestrial passage between two rivers—embodied the film's central metaphor. Though unable to identify the meaning of the *Molly Aida*'s journey over the mountain, Herzog has frequently emphasized that his entire filming project hinged on the image of a steamship leaving its normal habitat and being forced to do the unthinkable. There are good reasons to think of Herzog's obsession with this metaphor, in spite or precisely because of its reference to the philosophical figure of the sublime, as no less aesthetic and aestheticizing in intent than Fitzcarraldo's own effort to present engineering as a total work of art, as opera with other means. Early critics of the film surely saw no reason to differentiate between the protagonist and director and not to stress the association of both Fitzcarraldo's geography and Herzog's filming thereof with a deeply problematic conception of human exceptionalism. And yet, the last two decades and their writing about the concept of the Anthropocene, with their concern about the indelible footprints humans have left on planet Earth since the rise of industrial culture and the onset of the so-called "Great Acceleration"[3] in the early postwar period, offer numerous perspectives to rethink *Fitzcarraldo*'s geography. They urge us to think about the film's central metaphor not simply as a curious aberration of the aesthetic, as life becoming opera, but as a symptomatic cipher of an age in which formerly presumed boundaries between nature and culture, human and natural history, have lost their very hold.

Whether you date its beginnings to the invention of the steam engine in the late eighteenth century or to the dramatic increase in atmospheric carbon dioxide concentration after World War II, the concept of the Anthropocene has come to describe conditions under which human history and Earth history can no longer be separated, climate and human agency find themselves caught in reciprocal metabolisms, and we therefore can no longer think of history as being a purely intrahuman affair. Introduced by climate chemist Paul J. Crutzen in 2000, the notion of the Anthropocene was originally meant to describe the advent of a new geological epoch in which the impact of human activities on earth—humanity's geological, geochemical, atmospheric, and biological footprints—had categorically changed the history of the Earth itself. Whereas the relatively mild climactic conditions of the Holocene enabled the proliferation of human civilization and its firm (modern) belief in controlling nature, with the coming of the Anthropocene man-made climatic changes question long-held beliefs in humanity's physical and metaphysical authority over the natural world. According to Christophe Bonneuil and Jean-Baptiste Fressoz,

> The Anthropocene, as the reunion of human (historical) time and Earth (geological) time, between human agency and non-human agency, gives the lie to this—temporal, ontological, epistemological and institutional—great divide between nature and society that widened in the nineteenth and twentieth centuries. The new geohistorical epoch signals the irruption of the Earth (its temporality, its limits, its systemic dynamics) into what sought to be a history, an economy and a society emancipating themselves from natural constraints. It signals the return of the Earth into a world that Western industrial modernity on the whole represented to itself as above the earthly foundation. If our future involves a geological swing of the Earth into a new state, we can no longer believe in a humanity making its own history by itself.[4]

Initially caused by human efforts to control nature and change the course of Earth's deep temporalities, the Anthropocene's new entanglement of the human and the non-human therefore cannot but affect how we conceptualize the concept of the human. It urges us to revise long-held beliefs about the specificity and exceptionalism of the human species and its ability to steer its own path in the future. As Clive Hamilton summarizes, "This bizarre situation, in which we have become potent enough to change the course of the Earth yet seem unable to regulate ourselves, contradicts every modern belief about the kind of creature the human being is."[5]

Known during the film's production as the "trocha" (Spanish for path, shortcut, railway line), Herzog's and Fitzcarraldo's cut through the jungle no doubt embodied the very human arrogance that has established what we now have come to call the Anthropocene: man, to become man, must subject nature to his will, and in so doing defines the realms of the human and of the Earth as mutually exclusive. Though the clearing was to grow over again within a few years after the filming, Fitzcarraldo's geographical project situates the film's protagonist as a human paragon of the late Holocene: a willful agent eager to re-engineer the course of the Earth and its water systems, yet unable to consider the relationship of the human to the nonhuman, of culture to nature, as reciprocal, as part of a much larger metabolism. Fitzcarraldo's approach to the land is no different than his handling of this land's man-made map: all he can find when encountering the nonhuman is what humans, as they equate representation with strategies of power and control, have always already projected onto it. All he can recognize in the face of the other is a mirror image of himself.

Herzog's own thoughts about the trocha, as captured in Blank's *Burden of Dreams*, seem to strike a very different chord. They register the hubris, arrogance, and inevitable failure of late Holocene man to dominate or even remake the natural world. What Herzog, in a posture as unaffected as one can imagine, calls the obscenity and vileness of the jungle is meant to communicate the principle illegibility of the jungle, the fact that it cannot but remain exterior

Applied geography: The "Trocha."

to any effort on the part of humans to understand and project themselves onto the other. What Herzog considers the jungle's lack of order, its revengeful way of striking back at its human invaders, anticipates a world in which human-made climate change produces ever more violent weather conditions that belie any former ambitions to control nature. Unlike Fitzcarraldo, Herzog wants us to become humble vis-à-vis the jungle because humans cannot but fail in their efforts to recognize themselves in the natural world. He wants us to recognize our own limitations, our smallness and boundedness, so as to protect the human from any violent revenge of repressed nature against its thoughtless oppressors. In this, one could think of Herzog's jungle as a site staging a world- and earth-historical conflict between different conceptions of the human, between late Holocene visions of human progressivism and autonomy on the one hand, and on the other the Anthropocene's call for rethinking and reining in the human footprint on Earth.

Or so it seems at least. For Herzog's discovery of human smallness in the face of the presumed violence of the jungle—its crude eroticism, its moral depravity—is of course energized by nothing other than his quasi-Romantic aspiration to graft human features onto the nonhuman itself: he rhetorically proclaims the otherness of the natural world by imagining this other in terms of what is known and familiar. As a result, Herzog displays himself to be no more a critical sage or thinker of the Anthropocene than Fitzcarraldo. Both draw on old ontological juxtapositions of nature and culture, whereas the true challenge of our age of climate change and environmental catastrophes might be to rethink human agency in light of conditions in which human history and Earth history have become deeply entangled. Both Herzog and Fitzcarraldo suggest that humans, to become and be humans, must establish categorical divisions between mind and matter, the natural and the human-made, and in so doing forsake modes of thinking (and living) that draw any lessons from the complex interactions between spheres such as the atmosphere, biosphere, hydrosphere, and geosphere and the paths human societies believe to have carved out for themselves. In spite of their seemingly different stances, neither Kinski's Fitzcarraldo nor Herzog himself appear ready to revise their investments into human exceptionalism that has caused the rupture of the Anthropocene in the first place.

And yet, *Fitzcarraldo* itself seems to know something about this already, perhaps with, perhaps even against its maker's knowledge. Consider the following scene. As in the first half of the film the *Molly Aida*, much to Fitzcarraldo's crew's surprise, travels up rather than down the Amazon, Fitzcarraldo grows ever more anxious that his captain—the only crew member who knows about his general plan—might miss the proper turn off for the Rio Pachitea. The camera captures the following dialogue between captain and entrepreneur from a frontal perspective, visually emphasizing the cockpit's vertical window frame as if the two men inhabited two distinct realms of existence:

Fitzcarraldo: "We should have reached the Pachitea a long time ago."

Captain: "No, we haven't."

Fitzcarraldo: "But according to the map we have . . . "

Captain: "I don't rely on maps."

Fitzcarraldo: "How can you be so sure about that?"

Having panned left halfway through this dialogue to follow Fitzcarraldo's move into the captain's domain of the cockpit, the camera now suddenly cuts to a shot of the muddy waters of the Amazon, the ship's shadows visible on, yet also perturbed by, the very waves its passage leaves behind. Attached to a rope, a metal cup is filled with water, then pulled up. We cut to a close up of the captain. He tastes the water like a cook sampling his soup and then proclaims: "No river tastes like the Pachitea. It's just ahead of us."

For all his nervous agitation and determination, already at this early moment of his geographical project, Fitzcarraldo, with his

"No river tastes like the Pachitea."

maps, proves incapable of charting a reliable path. Herzog's camera leaves little doubt that human marks on paper—the power of representation, the imposition of culture as a separate realm onto nature—cannot but offer a flawed compass to navigate the land. We therefore should be warned about what is to come. Maps, we are told, do to human perception what imperial documents in *Aguirre* did to the colonizers' actions: they lead us astray, into the abyss of an imaginary, ultimately self-destructive sense of control. What is even more interesting about this sequence, however, is the way in which it invites the viewer to contemplate curious alternatives to Fitzcarraldo's understanding of geography. As he tastes the water to determine their location, the captain recognizes the complex metabolism that may exist between the human and the nonhuman. He literally takes in the water, samples it with his senses, so as to progress without abstracting himself from the land, without assuming a colonizer's "monarch-of-all-I-survey" perspective.[6] The scene stands out from the rest of the film, but it precisely for this reason deserves our full attention. Humans, in the captain's view, are deeply entangled with their environments; their bodies move and coevolve with other bodies, the matter of the world; their knowledge emanates not from the elevated platforms of culture and representation but from sensory interactions with the body of the Earth. With this, the captain, in however distorted form, serves today's viewers as a potent reminder that our age of the Anthropocene, in collapsing former divisions of nature and culture, may also generate what it might take to move beyond former conceptions of human exceptionalism, the arrogance of which led to this age's very rise and its looming catastrophes.

Flow

Fitzcarraldo's release sits on the cusp of a significant cultural and political watershed in then West Germany. Three months after the film's premiere, Rainer Werner Fassbinder's death marked the unraveling of New German Cinema, to which Herzog—in spite of his self-proclaimed outsider status—owed much of his national and international visibility. Ten months after the film first screened in West-German theaters, Helmut Kohl assumed his chancellorship, ending thirteen years of left-liberal rule and inaugurating a prolonged period of pervasive social and political conservatism, of widely perceived stagnation and tedium, cloaked in the rhetoric of a "spiritual-moral turn." And a little more than a year after the opening of the film, which like so many *auteur* films of the time relied heavily on government support and co-financing arrangements with the public broadcast channel ZDF (Zweites Deutsches Fernsehen), cable television was to hit the West-German market and rapidly and fundamentally change the topographies of audiovisual production, distribution, and consumption. *Fitzcarraldo*, of course, has no knowledge about how historical times would contract and transform after its making. And yet, in retrospect it is tempting to think of Herzog's project as a film in which German cinema took one final breath of creativity before political and cultural history imposed momentous changes.

It is tempting to consider the historical moment in which the plot of *Fitzcarraldo* takes place as one of ambivalence and unknowing anticipation as well. The production of rubber flourished around 1900 in the Amazon, situating a city such as Manaus as one of the wealthiest and "gaudiest cities in the world."[7] By 1910, however, after rubber seeds had been smuggled out of Brazil and Peru and started to thrive in other areas of the globe such as Malaysia, boom turned into bust, the rubber barons' opulence dwindled, and the regions' urban developments experienced decades of decay and utter poverty. What characterizes the history of rubber production of course also describes the history of European imperialism around 1900, of which Fitzcarraldo's effort to import opera to Iquitos might be seen as one (cultural) facet. The years after 1870 witnessed the largest acquisition of overseas territories by European empires in the entire history of Western colonialism, an unprecedented race to occupy foreign lands to exploit natural resources and create new markets. Though events such as the Berlin Conference of 1884–85 were meant to arbitrate the Western competition for colonial expansion, all of this of course exploded with the outbreak of World War I and was to lead to a momentous recalibration of global powers after 1918. Fitzcarraldo's operatic adventure thus transpires at a time of historic acceleration and contraction, of seeming mobility and expansion, that is pregnant with the elements of its imminent downfall and destruction. Like the making of the film itself, Fitzcarraldo's geographical project belongs to a historical period that in retrospect may have afforded (for some) a last glimpse of agency before various historical developments were to darken any future prospects.

Fitzcarraldo, its narrative as much as its very making, aspires to greatness amid what in the rear-view mirror of history has come to appear as a last-gasp moment of a distinct historical period. In his lectures on the philosophy of history, German philosopher G. W. F. Hegel famously defined historical greatness as the greatness of men who not only pursued self-proclaimed goals for individual gain, but followed "an unconscious impulse that occasioned the accomplishment of that for which the time was ripe."[8] For Hegel, great deeds require dynamics and logics that exceed an individual's control and willfulness. In his view, historical greatness manifests itself with a certain cunning of reason in whose absence any action, any effort to shape history, would merely appear abstract and empty of substance. Great men, in Hegel's historicist perspective, understand how to navigate the grey area between the intentional and the nonintentional. They know how to rub against the markers of their time in spite of the fact that they may fail to fully comprehend what they are doing. They act with great determination and at the same time allow the flow of things to do their work, strategize effectively to reach their goals, and trust their intuition.

Fitzcarraldo, no doubt, aspires to accomplish historical greatness. His plan to bring opera to the jungle is meant to achieve something for which his time is ripe without knowing it. As if sensing that history finds itself at the brink of decline and violent disintegration, his project resists the exigencies of the real and employs the operatic, on and off stage, as a medium to move history forward, as a metaphor of his desire to supersede historical stagnation. Mocked by the wealthy rubber barons after failing to garner their support, Fitzcarraldo—the horn of his gramophone under his arm, sweat on his forehead, rage in his eyes—confronts one of the Dons with the following tirade: "As true as I am standing here, one day I shall bring grand opera to Iquitos. I will outnumber you. I will outbillion you. I am the spectacle in the forest. I am the inventor of rubber. I will outrubber you. Sir, the reality of your world is nothing more than a rotten caricature of great opera." The bringing of real opera to Iquitos, in Fitzcarraldo's feverish vision, is to inaugurate no less than a new era of history. It will obliterate the current regime of self-indulgence, replacing mere facades and decaying caricatures of life with true expressions of grandeur and meaning. As if he were a rather impatient student of both Hegelian dialectics and Wagner's writing on art, Fitzcarraldo's hope is to mobilize the idea of grand opera against its present shapes so as to infuse history with new vitality and beat a doomed present at its own game.

Hardcore Hegelians will see little reason to consider Fitzcarraldo's actions as signs of individual, let alone historical, greatness: his is a life of undue willfulness, so obstinate and headstrong, so ruthless in its pursuits, that he can't help but fail to measure the pulse of his time, even unconsciously. In the actions of great men, a time's and a person's unconscious join forces to endow individual ambitions with compelling force. Fitzcarraldo might be a dreamer in Herzog's sense, a believer in operatic world-making, but in his zealous effort to make and mark history, he shows no trust in the cunning of what exceeds his control and awareness, he has no tolerance for how any psychological or social unconscious could energize his schemes. And yet, in spite of his strained attentiveness, his unconditional presence and dedication to his vision, we repeatedly witness Fitzcarraldo in moments of curious absentmindedness, of distraction and drift—moments in which intuition and nonintentionality seem to take hold over him, align his impulsiveness with larger dynamics, and somehow manage to suspend the pace of goal-oriented action. Consider the scene in which Fitzcarraldo beholds the map of the area and its rivers in Don Auqilino's office. Reminded by Don Auqilino of the fateful expedition of 1896 and then asked whether he has ever seen any shrunken heads, Fitzcarraldo answers inattentively: "Yes . . . I mean . . . ." His head briefly turns toward his interlocutor, yet his eyes and mind remain somewhere else. The pause in his response is telling: a symptom of repressed knowledge, expressing a clear disjunct between the discursive and the non-discursive.[9] Though he should attend to ample signs of warning, his fancy is already carrying him up the river. While his words feign common understanding, their automatism and the pause between them mark them as elements of a language of the unconscious, as signs at once recognizing and masking what Fitzcarraldo's ambition displaces from view. Consider a later scene during the trip up the Pachitea in which Fitzcarraldo, his head turned toward the rear of the ship while the captain gazes forward to pilot the vessel, discovers the sudden presence of hundreds of Indians behind them who block any possible return route. Thomas Mauch's camera captures Kinski's stare for seconds on end before it finally, with a reverse shot, shows what our protagonist physically sees. None of what we can possibly detect in Fitzcarraldo's eyes, however, evidences any recognition of possible danger. His gaze is one of awe and captivation, it attends closely to what populates the visual field, but it at the same time features something dreamlike and registers some sense of incredulity—as if our protagonist found himself in a curious space of ambiguity between the real and the surreal, the conscious and the unconscious, control and drift.

Fitzcarraldo's inattentiveness.

Whenever signs of divided attention, of drift and distraction, seize Fitzcarraldo's mien, our protagonist enters a temporal twilight zone markedly different from the spasms of historical time that structure his contemporary moment. He resides both in and outside time. He intensely attends—stretches—to what is present before him, yet he at the same time approaches the Now as a mere portal to a categorically different future. While seemingly occupied with schemes and strategies that elude his interlocutors, he cannot help but follow the drive and mandates of his intuition, of something transcending the boundaries of sovereign subjectivity. Fitzcarraldo is agent and medium at once, centered and decentered, inattentive and hyperattentive. Which is perhaps just another way of saying that he, in spite of all his desire to shape, control, and command the real and do to the world what artists do to clay, at heart he is simply a man of flow, of what Mihaly Csikszentmihaly calls optimal experience.[10]

Unlike other mental states such as anxiety, apathy, arousal, boredom, control, relaxation, and worry, the concept of flow, according to Csikszentmihalyi, describes a way of experiencing skillful activities in play, art, ritual, work, or sports as if they were utterly intuitive and effortless. To experience flow relies on the sense that our skill levels are adequate to the challenge levels at hand: "Concentration is so intense that there is no attention left over to think about anything irrelevant, or to worry about problems. Self-consciousness disappears, and the sense of time becomes distorted. An activity that produces such experiences is so gratifying that people are willing to do it for its own sake, with little concern for what they will get out of it, even when it is difficult, or dangerous."[11] Though it is difficult to say exactly what his skill set might be, Herzog's Fitzcarraldo aspires to a life in which flow figures as a permanent condition of existence. His modus operandi is to pursue self-chosen goals fully immersed in and energized by feelings of utter focus and determination, even though his intensity may register as a state of absentmindedness or distraction in the eyes of others. Goal-oriented intentionality and intuitive action, utter attentiveness and loss of self-consciousness, danger and apparent effortless for him go hand in hand. He may pursue outrageous plans for particular reasons, but in the end he may just do so for a particular action's own sake, for maintaining an ongoing sense of flow. As a result, Fitzcarraldo's sense of time, of being and navigating temporality, fundamentally differs from that of his fellow travelers. He vanishes into the funnels of time rather than controls or triumphs over them. He disappears into history, its crises and contractions, instead of imposing himself as a lynchpin of historical transformations.

Critics have discussed Fitzcarraldo's relation to trees as key to understanding his persona, his colonial ambitions. He anxiously stares at the jungle when traveling down the river, constantly expecting the sudden appearance of native enemies eager to rebut his incursion. Trees, for him, at once obscure and embody the very Other his journey provokes. Later, he fells trees, not simply in order to cut a path for his steamship, but to exorcise the fears he projects onto the forest, to eradicate his self-incurred but real paranoia and

Fitzcarraldo and the trees.

do away with possible causes for any violent return of the repressed. Fitzcarraldo's relation to trees thus features him as a subject in painstaking need to control and contain at all costs not simply the world around him but also his innermost desires and fears. But over the last decades, critics, in primarily discussing the metaphor Herzog himself wanted us to see as the film's pivot, might have lost sight of some of the forest for the trees. For how does our reading of the film change if we think of Fitzcarraldo not simply as a protagonist engaged in a rather quixotic struggle with the jungle, but as a man navigating and making amends with the flow of Amazonian water in both material and metaphorical terms? What if we, contrary to Herzog, focused more on Fitzcarraldo's relationship to water and its flows, and, by extension, on the *Molly Aida*'s course along different rivers, as the film's primary visual and narrative axis, and thus shifted some of our attention away from Fitzcarraldo's haunted effort to make the steamship leave its habitat, its normal ecosystem?

"Ecosystems," writes Veronica Strang, "whether local, regional or planetary in scale, [require] a particular hydraulic balance—the right amount of water, at the right pace, and at the right time. So, at all levels, water's life-giving potential relies not only on its properties, but also on a carefully balanced flow in its movements."[12] The decades building up to Fitzcarraldo's operatic and geographical project saw many European efforts to re-engineer aquatic flows, be it in the form of re-routing entire riverbeds for the sake of improved traffic and flood control, be it in the form of dams constructed for irrigation purposes. Rampant industrialization went hand in hand with a recalibration and, in many respects, unsettling of the balance of the Earth's hydraulic systems. Fitzcarraldo enters the film quite attuned to what Europeans, whether colonizing other or reworking their own lands, did to nature's water flows. Though he fails to monetize his ambition, we get to know him as a pioneer of ice production. He not only understands how to make use of water's unique molecular composition, its capacity to physically transform from fluid to steam or fluid to ice. As importantly, Fitzcarraldo's initial effort is no less than to trade in water as a solid, to cast its amorphousness into manageable forms, to arrest its flows and make it pliable to human will, desire, and need. Similar to many nineteenth-century engineers, Fitzcarraldo enters Herzog's film with the understanding that to control the flow and shape of water, to redefine the hydraulic balance, is to hold power and gain influence.

The first dialogue in Herzog's 1972 *Aguirre* has the film's protagonist—with the muddy waters of an Amazon tributary cascading in the background—proclaim: "Now it's going downhill." It doesn't take much to realize that Kinski's words are meant to be both literal and metaphorical in nature; the float along and down the river turns out to be a voyage into European colonialism's heart of darkness. *Fitzcarraldo*'s aquatic politics are quite different. They undergo various phases. After the protagonist's trade in frozen water has not produced its desired profits, Fitzcarraldo's *Molly Aida* first travels up the Pachitea, at which point the plot's pacing enters a mode of roaming and assumes the kind of episodic openness

Fitzcarraldo and the shapes of water.

typically associated with the road-movie genre. Once the mountain has been traversed, the ship—unmoored by the Indians—rumbles through the rapids of the Pongo das Mortes, its hulk banging hard against rocks left and right, its passengers thrown across the deck, water gushing uncontrollably, the camera capturing the events as if all this was part of a documentary feature. Things continue to go downstream and hence downhill from here, yet in dramatic contrast to the itinerary of *Aguirre*, Fitzcarraldo's river journey becomes one not into darkness, but into a kind of equilibrium, a realm of flow Csikszentmihalyi would call optimal experience. As the *Molly Aida* approaches Iquitos in the film's final minutes, Fitzcarraldo has literally and metaphorically learned how to go with the flow. While his hired ensemble intones *I Puritani* and thus fulfills the historical avant-garde's dream of obliterating the boundaries between art and life, Fitzcarraldo is shown to be in the zone—like a skillful basketball player navigating the paint seemingly without effort and conscious reflection. He no longer struggles against hostile currents, rapids, and given hydraulic forces; there is no more need to mobilize attention for the sake of mastering the unmasterable, of making or shaping history as if it were made of clay. He is no longer fighting to undo and remake aquatic balances. Rather than to impose his willfulness onto the course of Amazonian waters, his return to Iquitos features him as a subject curiously in sync with his ecosystem: a subject deeply attuned to the reciprocity of the human and the nonhuman, the agency and flow of all matter. Fitzcarraldo may not return to Iquitos in the posture of what Hegel would call a great man, yet his body language radiates the simultaneous bliss of feeling recognized by and recognizing the world he has come to call his. It is difficult not to think of Fitzcarraldo, as he at the end of his Odyssey tunes into both the sounds of grand opera and the drift of the river, as a happy person.

A glimpse of happiness.

The Sounds of Music

It is finally time to address what *Fitzcarraldo* at heart is all about, namely the power of sound and music to express emotions, channel desire, connect different bodies, minds, and souls, and—most importantly—build alternate worlds within and in opposition to the dreary routines of the real. *Fitzcarraldo* ends with music from Verdi's *I Puritani* many seconds after the screen has turned black already; the film opens to the ethereal sounds of Popul Vuh, the German ethnic avant-garde band founded by Florian Fricke, here endowing grainy images of the jungle with metaphysical texture and depth. What unfolds in between leaves little doubt that *Fitzcarraldo*, as much as it serves as a vehicle of striking images and hallucinatory visions, offers a laboratory probing the effects of audible sound, of melody and rhythm, of voice and musical timbre, on the fabrics of human life and the boundaries of the subject. "Music," Arthur

Schopenhauer wrote in the early nineteenth century, "expresses in an exceedingly universal language, in a homogeneous material, that is, in mere tones, and with the greatest distinctness and truth, the inner being, the in-itself, of the world, which we think of under the concept of will, according to its most distinct manifestation."[13] *Fitzcarraldo* puts Schopenhauer's proposition to the test. Music, in Herzog's film, is a serious matter precisely because it seems to elude matter and representation and taps into resources that exceed vision's association with control, distance, rationality, and disembodiment. Whether it is really as universal and homogenous as Schopenhauer suggests, however, remains *Fitzcarraldo*'s open question.

Herzog's passion for opera is well-known. Many of his films spurt operatic soundtracks, some of his work tackles the history of European opera head-on, and repeatedly Herzog has directed operas for different theatrical venues himself. And yet, our first encounter with the world of opera in *Fitzcarraldo*—Verdi's *Ernani*, as staged in the opera house at Manaus and attended by Fitzcarraldo and Molly after an excruciating trip down the Amazon—certainly eludes the seriousness music typically claims in Herzog's work.[14] Campily staged by Werner Schroeter, this opening sequence, particularly the depiction of Sarah Bernhardt, borders on the farcical and ridiculous. In Schroeter's staging, Bernhardt is being mimed on stage by another actress while she herself remains clearly visible below the stage. This female stand-in, in all her effort to steal the show, is clearly played by a male performer, perhaps to underscore the extraterritoriality associated with the presence of European opera in the Amazon jungle. Meanwhile, we witness Enrico Caruso visibly annoyed and distracted by the gaudy gestures of the false Bernhardt, so much so that his own suicide scene loses some of its dramatic traction. The opening sequence of *Fitzcarraldo* thus stages *Ernani* as a drama in which utter artifice displaces artistry, eccentricity rules over emotion, superficiality drowns out any sign of truth and authenticity. None of this, however, seems to disturb Fitzcarraldo, whose tousled hair and

Caruso in Manaus: "He is pointing at me . . . he means me."

oil-stained suit mark him as an outsider amid the audience. His sole concern is Caruso's vocal brilliance. As Caruso in the role of Ernani sinks the dagger into his chest and—his arms outstretched like Fitzcarraldo's in the much later sequence above the trees—falls to his knees, Fitzcarraldo believes himself to be seen and acknowledged by Caruso. With his eyes wide open, he stares in the direction of the stage and whispers excitedly to Molly: "He is pointing at me ... he means me."

While the visual staging and performative excess of *Ernani* marks opera as preposterous, the sounds of Caruso's voice and the bodily gestures it activates define music as a realm of unique recognition and resonance, of touching upon and being touched by what appears to be physically separate. In spite of many signs indicating the contrary, music in *Fitzcarraldo* therefore does much more than simply serve as a vessel of self-expression, a site to articulate or stir grand emotions, a mechanism to subject listeners to mindless awe and sublime self-denial. Nor can we think of opera here merely as an imperial instrument of power: an apparatus enabling European willfulness to triumph over the colonial other, Western melody over indigenous rhythmicality, Verdi and Bellini over the Amazon's auditory cultures. Rather than simply function as a channel of communication, music in *Fitzcarraldo* instead embodies no less than a medium according to the more elemental understanding of media as "vessels and environments, containers of possibility that anchor our existence and make what we are doing possible."[15] Similar to how early modern thinkers considered air, water, fire, and earth as media because they offered environments enabling diverse forms of life, so does *Fitzcarraldo* approach the sounds and reverberations of music as curious ensembles of nature and culture, the elemental and human craft—as aesthetic infrastructures offering shared conditions for life, interaction, and mutual recognition. Once stripped of its performative artifice, music in sum wants to foreshadow and even model possible worlds governed by nonhierarchical relationships. It

"Now it's Caruso's turn."

invites humans to share environments with other humans, or even nonhumans, that are void of violence, coercion, and repression.

Consider one of the film's signature scenes, which—captured as still image—has often been used to advertise the film. Fitzcarraldo and his by-now decimated crew have just left the missionary station; the *Molly Aida* continues to head upstream toward inhospitable lands along the Pachitea. Suddenly, the sounds of persistent drumming and chanting envelop the ship, causing everyone on board to stare with anxious eyes at the passing jungle and direct their guns at what eludes their sight. The captain orders the engine be slowed down, thus emulating the curious suspension of narrative time and progress we as viewers experience during this sequence. After chief engineer Cholo ignites some dynamite to scare the drummers and chanters, the sounds indeed cease for a moment, triggering the captain to remark: "There are silences and silences. And this one, I don't like at all." Before long, the rhythmic drumming and chanting kicks in again and raises the crew's anxiety to new levels even though—or precisely because—their intense gazing at the banks of the river continuously fails to identify possible foes. We cut to Fitzcarraldo standing on top of the ship's superstructure. He places his gramophone on a stand, hectically turns the turntable's crank.[16] "Now it's Caruso's turn," he pronounces right before the voice of the famous tenor intones "Il sogno" from Jules Massenet's *Manon* (1882), an aria in which the opera's male protagonist details a dream of happiness, to be achieved by his lover's presence in a beautiful landscape. While the recording's scratchy singing fills the scenery and adds a second acoustical layer on top of the Indian's acousmatic sounds, Herzog's cuts to a medium shot of Fitzcarraldo standing behind his phonograph. His right hand rests gently on the apparatus. His head turns left and right. His eyes are wide open. His attention levels are elevated to the max. Eventually the drumming subsides, as if yielding to Caruso's mechanically reproduced presence, while Fitzcarraldo's body and hand arch slightly backwards. His pose signals what he senses as the success of his intervention: the silencing of ominous native sounds with the help of Western harmony and melody, the taming of wild nature through advanced culture and technology.

Or so it seems, at least. It is quite plausible to read the action as an act of acoustical colonialism realized through lopsided channels of communication. It not only presents Italian opera as eliminating the rhythms of indigenous cultures, but renders the Amazon's native Indians—similar to the mythic audiences of early cinema—as being unable to distinguish between the real and its technological reproduction and hence deeply susceptible to what Fitzcarraldo broadcasts to them. A slight adjustment of perspective, however, should bring us to somewhat different conclusions, perhaps more benign, perhaps even more precarious in nature. Opera, for Fitzcarraldo, is not a mere missionary tool with which to imprint his will and vision onto other people, be they rubber barons, the children of Iquitos, or the Jívaros along the river. Though Caruso's voice is shown to work on Fitzcarraldo's own emotions like a hand modeling clay, Fitzcarraldo's ambition when disseminating the tenor's singing in the jungle is to retune his entire environment. For him, opera is a way of being in the world. It provides an infrastructure defining the entire relationship of humans to each other and to their found or built surroundings; an immersive cocoon that knows of no outside; a scaffolding that makes human interaction possible in the first place. Rather than sending messages meant to convert the listener to appreciate Western culture, opera creates entire atmospheres— sonorous horizons of experience in whose context sentient beings can resonate with each other and develop new types of attachments. Caruso's voice, in Fitzcarraldo's perspective, therefore has the power to build entire new worlds instead of simply recalibrating some of the existing world's elements. It envelops and remodels the senses and thereby lays the groundwork for nonviolent encounters and associations, for a new attuning of mind and matter.

Critical theorists will not hesitate to dissect Fitzcarraldo's understanding of opera as an elemental medium of resonance. For them, to retune the entire sensible world with the help of Western music might in fact be even worse than the effort to block possible channels of communication and silence one source of sound with the help of another. It would mean remaking the other in the image (or better: the sound) of the self and establishing what is culturally particular in the name of deeply ideological claims for universality. And yet, as we know from the history of thought, even the most transparent ideologies of universal meaning typically contain transformative energies that at some future moment may empower precisely those whose voice the mantras of universalism initially silenced. Nineteenth-century workers' movements turned the bourgeoisie's ideological quest for universal freedom against itself; suffragettes claimed the very right to vote men had once declared as a cornerstone of democratic societies yet had solely reserved for themselves. A somewhat more generous reading of Fitzcarraldo's politics of resonance might therefore not simply expose its ideological blindfold, but elaborate on its utopian urgency, its spark of generative power that may become fully readable only to some future generation.

Fitzcarraldo's understanding of opera as a retuning of the world embraces sound and hearing as media of ephemerality that suspend vision's putative stress on distance and detachment, vision's privileged role in Western conceptions of control, truth, and self-reflexivity. Hearing, at least in Fitzcarraldo's understanding, does not provide the privilege of meta-positions; it cannot do without the physical proximity of the listener and what is heard, a certain sense of sharing time and space, the reciprocal immanence of touching and being touched by the vibrant properties of sound. An entire ecology of perception rather than a mere message transported from sender to received, Fitzcarraldo's opera—in Salomé Voegelin's words written in a different context—"necessitates an involved participation ... and the object or event under consideration is by necessity considered not as an artefact but in its dynamic production. This is a continual production that involves the listener as intersubjectively constituted in perception, while producing the very thing he perceives, and both, the subject and the work, thus generated concomitantly, are as transitory as each other."[17] According to the film's protagonist, Caruso's voice is meant to invite the Jívaros to acts of involved participation. Their silence is no act of surrender. It in fact testifies to the extent to which music—as an ecology of perception—decenters received notions of sovereignty, combative identity, and goal-orientated agency. However ideological its universalism, opera in *Fitzcarraldo* privileges process over product, the ephemerality of touch over the power of distant observation. It promises a world in which subject and object, perceiver and perceived, matter and mind, co-constitute and resonate with each other—a world that suspends the kind of strategic subjectivity that has fueled imperial politics as much as the systematic ravaging of the Earth.

Opera and sound, in Herzog's *Fitzcarraldo*, pushes against and beyond the limits of representation and signification. If we simply assess it as a complex of signs, as a delivery machine for imperial meanings, we will fail to understand its role. Though it is tempting to ask: "What does music in *Fitzcarraldo* mean and what does it represent amid the encounter of different cultural traditions?," the more adequate and pertinent questions are: "What does music do, how does it operate, what kind of processes does its materially inflect and effectuate?" Sound here is not bound to its source—that is, Fitzcarraldo's gramophone—as this source's property. It instead has its own life and vibrancy, its own force and flow. It acts on, sets in motion, or arrests other matter and thus renders audible, as Christoph Cox argues in his reading of Nietzsche's writing on music, "the dynamic, differential, discordant flux of becoming that precedes and exceeds empirical individuals."[18]

It is for this reason that *Fitzcarraldo*'s final sequence, as it stages the protagonist's operatic return to Iquitos, may also afford more generous views than most critics have been willing to grant. As indicated earlier, the film's final minutes feature Fitzcarraldo—in the posture of a grand impresario—reveling in the performance of a makeshift opera ensemble on board the *Molly Aida* while the residents of Iquitos are shown waving at the approaching steamship. Fitzcarraldo, who in a previous scene had asserted that Wagner's music speaks little to him, here comports himself at first as if his sole project had been to consolidate the jungle into a new Bayreuth, a self-contained total work of art rather than a malleable ecology of sensory perception. However, in looking closely at this scene and at how music here effects matter and movement, we should doubt whether the film really endorses this impression. First of all, it is quite obvious that Fitzcarraldo owes his bliss not simply to the staging of Bellini's *I Puritani*, but also to his own visibility on board the moving steamship. Fitzcarraldo's operatic intervention thus turns out to be hardly as totalizing as we may want to at first assume: it requires external reference points without whose existence the entire scene and performance would collapse. Second, it is difficult not to notice

Opera on the move.

that Herzog, in the final moments of *Fitzcarraldo*, initially refuses to provide any images that show ship and audience in one and the same frame, and then allows Bellini's music to continue even after the screen no longer shows any images at all anymore. The effect of Herzog's very deliberate editing is less that the ship and the shore come across as ontologically separate worlds than that we come to recognize image and music as something that could never add up to a totalizing and self-contained Wagnerian whole at all. At once literally on the move and metaphorically moving its listeners, what enables music to act on the world in *Fitzcarraldo*'s final moments also empowers sound to pierce the frames of cinematic vision and undo any frame's effort to represent the real as a sequence of self-contained impressions.

Unlike Wagner's dream, then, visuality and music at the end of Herzog's *Fitzcarraldo* do not fuse into one integrated whole: the moving ecology of audible sound is not and can never be co-extensive with the world of framed vision. While Fitzcarraldo himself in the end may interpret his own life as a unified representation and embodiment of grand opera, the editing of Herzog's film insists that opera at its best is about ceaseless flux and becoming, a postrepresentational dynamic in which different bodies, vibrations, forces, and logics of movement act on each other and thereby unsettle our conception of a self-contained work of art.

On Dangerous Grounds

Numerous stories about how Herzog placed undue burdens on actors and extras during the shooting of *Fitzcarraldo* have haunted the film ever since its making. Though Herzog has not denied the risks he took to complete the film, he at the same time has repeatedly justified his decision not to resort to elaborate special effects as critical to the film's success. Unrelenting location work with his principal actors, for him, was as important as heaving a real ship of 320 tons across a mountain in order to achieve the most compelling product. Though the final film—all claims to the contrary—includes a few seconds of footage in which a model of the Molly Aida maneuvers down studio-built rapids,[19] in Herzog's perspective, neither the use of miniature plastic boats nor the controlled environment of a studio could have yielded comparable results. What is intriguing about Herzog's insistence on filming in the face of risk, danger, and exhaustion, however, is the fact that none of this—contrary to common assumption—was done for the sake of amplifying the film's sense of realism. According to Herzog's understanding, authenticity and realism do not necessarily share the same ground. The latter describes a certain language of filmmaking, a mode of representing the world; the former identifies what drives the production of viable aesthetic work in the first place, the engine and fuel that makes great art possible no matter how frenzied, mad, or outrageous it may appear to the viewer. In one of his conversations with Paul Cronin, Herzog explained: "When the boat is crashing through the rapids it jerks the gramophone so that suddenly we hear opera music playing, and all the realistic noises fade away to reveal Caruso singing. And at the end of the film, once the boat starts to move, there are fewer and fewer people in the shot. It is almost as if the boat were gliding by its own force over the top. Had we shown anyone it would have been a realistic event, an event of human labour. As it is, the whole thing has been transformed into an operatic event of fever dreams and pure imagination, a highly stylized and grandiose scene of jungle fantasies."[20]

In her recent writing on special effects in the age of computer-generated imagery, Kristen Whissel has coined the term "effects emblem" to describe special effects that, in spite of their task of eliciting sensations of speechless awe, do not rupture the flow of narrative time.[21] In contemporary digital cinema, the role of spectacular images and photorealistic renditions of extreme vertical extensions, of human multitudes, of strange creatures and morphing human bodies is both to visualize the central theme and the narrative stakes of films such as *Avatar*, the *Lord of the Rings* trilogy, *Jurassic Park*, or *The Matrix*. They take on narrative functions instead of simply catering to the audience's hunger for non-narrative attractions.

Shot long before the advent of CGI, Herzog's *Fitzcarraldo*—in its very refusal to employ elaborate special effects in the name of producing impressions of authenticity—certainly knows a thing or two about what it means to offer astonishing images for the sake of emblematizing rather than suspending the flow of cinematic storytelling. While it is questionable to insist that the journey of the *Molly Aida* was captured without the use of any special effects, including the special effect that is cinema in and of itself, the ship's dangerous path over the mountain and down the rapids no doubt provides—like CGI effects in contemporary blockbuster cinema—a site, in the words of Kristen Whissel, "of intense signification" that "gives stunning (and sometimes) allegorical impression to a film's key themes, anxieties, and conceptual obsessions—*even as it provokes feelings of astonishment and wonder*."[22] Neither Herzog nor his protagonist, neither Herzog's viewers circa 1982 nor contemporary spectators may exactly know what the steamship's awe-inspiring trajectory is meant to mean. What is quite clear, however, is the fact that the image of the ship, in both facing and producing a whole series of dangerous events, is there to emblematize the narrative stakes of the film as a whole and thus serve as one of *Fitzcarraldo*'s principal engines of storytelling. Contrary to what we have come to learn about the opposition of early cinemas of attraction and narrative integration,[23] the cinematic spectacle of risk and danger in *Fitzcarraldo*—however stylized and operatic—is key to the film's narrative ambitions as well.

Film scholars might draw on two different historical approaches to discuss the emblematic role of risk and danger in the filming of *Fitzcarraldo*. André Bazin's work of the mid-twentieth century suggests that we should understand Herzog's voyage on dangerous grounds as an effort to reveal the ontological realism of the cinematic medium and embrace a rhetoric of simplicity, purity, and transparency. Cameras, Bazin once argued, may not always be able to witness and capture the most hazardous events of geographical exploration. In "offering fluid and trembling images"[24] of the general action, however, what they can do, as in the case of *Kon-Tiki* (1950), is to offer quasi-objective indices of a protagonist's perception, agitation, or memory; what cameras, by participating in a certain adventure, are able to record best and most truthfully are danger's effects on the human sensorium rather than its physical causes. Ernst Jünger's writing on photography around 1930 provides another perspective. For Jünger, photographic images of dangerous events—warfare, the perilous speed of modern industrial life—provided a training ground for the art of cool conduct; they enabled the twentieth-century subject to develop a second consciousness untouched by the potential shocks of modern existence and thus, by defining the camera's artificial eye as the truth and essence of organic vision, beat processes of modern alienation and objectification at their own game. "The act of taking a photograph stands outside the zone of sensibility. It has a telescope character: one realizes that the event is seen by an impervious and invulnerable eye. It captures both the flight of the bullet and the man at the moment in which he is torn apart by the explosion. This, however, is our specific manner of seeing, and photography is nothing other than an instrument of the peculiarity."[25]

In challenging Herzog's explicit desire to film under challenging conditions, critics have often read—directly or by implication—Herzog's quest for authenticity as a foray into Bazinian realism or Jüngerian cold conduct. The risks Herzog takes, according to this understanding, are meant either to tease intense performances out of his actors and produce images whose veracity will not be questioned by the audience; or to expose both himself and his future audiences to forms of looking that unsettle how Western culture has implicated the gaze in various regimes of identification, empathy, and desire. It is not difficult to see that these two positions, in spite of sharing certain phenomenological underpinnings, are mutually exclusive: the first considers danger as a medium that makes possible a descent into the deepest recesses of what it means to be human; the second embraces hazardous moments as sites to overcome human vulnerability and inaugurate an era of technologically driven posthumanism.

What is more important for our context here, however, is to understand that neither of these two positions really do justice to Herzog's politics of authenticity in *Fitzcarraldo*. Herzog's point is not just to capture images audiences will recognize not to be products of trick photography and postproduction tampering. Nor is it to challenge the viewer's perception with images that assimilate human perception to the operations of mechanical vision. Instead, Herzog's principal ambition is first of all to use his camera—unlike the realist or naturalist—to build and present alternate rather than re-present existing worlds, including the feverish dreams of mad conquerors and obstinate entrepreneurs in the jungle. He not only embraces the contingencies of location shooting to generate images that defy expectation and thereby activate wondrous stories-to-be-told. In engaging with the contingent and intractable, he also aspires to invite viewers to see the hitherto unseen and in so doing change us and our seeing itself. Second, Herzog's mode of athletic filmmaking is one that—in contrast to the advocates of cold conduct—hopes to intensify rather than obliterate the viewer's experience. It wants to unsettle conventional borders between subject and object, not in order to absorb the individual into the mechanical operations of a technology-driven world, but to expand subjectivity and thereby reshuffle the gravity and normativity of the real. In Blank's *Burden of Dreams*, Herzog may indeed often sound utterly cold and detached when speaking about the challenges of filming *Fitzcarraldo* in the jungle. All things told, however, Herzog's coldness may have registered no more and no less than the toll it takes to simultaneously (and therefore perhaps: foolishly) dispute

64

Athletic filmmaking (*Burden of Dreams*).

seasoned humanist concepts of realism and the untimely lures of techno-posthumanism.

None of this will alleviate concerns critics have raised about Herzog's presence in the jungle, his use and abuse of indigenous people in pursuing his project, the hazardous privileging of authenticity over make-believe. Even though—contrary to initial reports—no one was killed as a direct result of the actual shooting of the film, and even though the more than 700 Indians involved in the filming were to receive legal title to their lands and be protected from the inroads of powerful gas and oil drilling companies, Herzog's auteurial politics of authenticity remain no doubt problematic. To think that no good art exists without taking certain risks is one thing. To exploit pain, suffering, and exhaustion as catalysts of aesthetic stylization is quite another. What is interesting to note, however, is the fact that *Fitzcarraldo* itself seems to know all too well about what critics often found lacking in Herzog's own reflection about the making of the film. The film on the one hand leaves little doubt about the fact that Fitzcarraldo's quest for authenticity cannot do without the performative aspects of his character. He pretends to be the white-haired god of Jívaros mythology to muster their collaboration in spite of the fact that the Indians are fully aware of his dissimulation, his act of make-believe. He knows that they know that he is not the real thing, and yet everyone silently agrees to move forward in their hope to dominate the land. On the other hand, in his embodiment of the film's protagonist, Klaus Kinski offers ample evidence of the precarious status of humanist subjectivity, that is, the extent to which modern technology, science, and rationality, including the modernity of technological vision and filmic recording, unsettle any quest for authentic subjecthood. Throughout the film, Kinski is playing Kinski as much as he is playing Fitzcarraldo. No sequence seems to pass without him seeking to engage the camera in a double entendre, to

A white-haired God?

speak with two voices at once: to diegetic as much as non-diegetic audiences.

Consider a short, albeit emblematic, scene towards the end of the film. Cut loose by the Jívaros, the *Molly Aida* has just passed the dangerous waters of the Pongo das Mortes contrary to its owner's intention. We witness Fitzcarraldo, at his wits' end, back at Don Aquilino's plantation, a few miles downstream from Iquitos. Our protagonist is about to sell his steamship to the rubber baron and thus seal the failure of his venture into rubber extraction and opera patronage. A close-up shows Kinski poised at a window, the window's frame offering a view on the quiet waters of the Amazon as much as it frames Fitzcarraldo himself. "I'll tell you a story," he addresses Don Aquilino, briefly turning his head to the right before contemplating the sight of the river again. "At the time when North America was hardly explored, one of those early French trappers went westwards from Montreal and he was the first white man to set eyes on Niagara Falls. When he returned, he told of waterfalls that were more vast and immense than people had ever dreamed of. But no one believed him. They thought he was a madman or a liar. They asked him, 'What's your proof?' And he answered: 'My proof is that I have seen them.'" We cut to a medium close-up of Don Aquilino, his face communicating both bewilderment about and some sense of empathy with our storyteller telling stories about other storytellers. We cut back to a close-up of Fitzcarraldo, the eye lines of both men presumably meeting each other. "Sorry, I don't really know what that's got to do with me," we hear Fitzcarraldo utter, his head turned toward the window again, right before another cut shows us both men in front of the entire set of windows that separate house and river and define architecture as an aperture onto the transitoriness of nature.

Almost two decades after the making of *Fitzcarraldo* Werner Herzog would declare in his infamous *Minnesota Manifesto*: "There are deeper strata of truth in cinema, and there is such a thing as

"I'll tell you a story."

poetic, ecstatic truth. It is mysterious and elusive, and can be reached only through fabrication and imagination and stylization."[26] Fitzcarraldo's French trapper anticipates Herzog's assault on what he understands to be cinema verité. This trapper has no material proof of what he has witnessed, no indexical record documenting his experience. What he has are vibrant impressions and memories, strata of experience more powerful than what accountants or historians expect as evidence. What he has are words that stylize the imprint of the natural sublime into a captivating story. His truth about seeing the wonders of Niagara Falls is truly ecstatic in Herzog's later sense. It relies not on a subject's megalomaniacal effort to declare himself the center of the world, but on the contrary on how this world with all its gravity resonates with this subject's modes of sensory perception and thereby decenters his or her ordinary filters and hierarchies of cognition. The trapper's eyes are to the falls what silver halide crystals in photographic film are to light waves and particles entering a camera. They register spectacular sights without will or intention, they allow the material world to imprint itself onto the trapper's mind and imagination while bypassing the distortions of subjective willfulness, and it is precisely for this reason that the trapper's story contains more truth and evidentiary force than any physical document or secondary account could ever deliver. Subjectivity, in Herzog, bears the ecstatic burden of truth whenever it happens to serve as a resonant echo chamber of the world.

What does the trapper's story have to do with Fitzcarraldo himself and how Kinski embodies him for us? During the telling of the trapper's story, Herzog's camera shows Fitzcarraldo mostly from the back, his gaze fastened on the landscape outside the window. Fitzcarraldo is a viewer of framed visions, not that different from how his audience—we—view him on screen. And yet, due to the angle of the camera, Fitzcarraldo's head obscures considerable portions of the window pane, thus suggesting a certain permeability and ambiguity of its frame. Fitzcarraldo, as framed by Herzog, appears as part of the distant image framed by the window: he represents either a framed framer of stories or an active membrane allowing viewed spaces to touch upon the space of viewing. No matter how we read his position, his body mediates between fore- and background, between image and the "real," interior and exterior spaces, the static and the transitory, physical presence and the imagination. Throughout most of the telling of the trapper's story, Fitzcarraldo stares through the window though his head will repeatedly veer slightly off to the right so as to gesture his awareness of or eagerness for being heard. However, Kinski's head turns dramatically away from the window and toward the camera at precisely the moment when Fitzcarraldo's story of the trapper's story reaches the central theme of evidence: "My proof is that I have seen them." Kinski's eyes after his turn do not directly meet the gaze of the camera; they look past it to what we must presume to be the location of his inner-diegetic listener, Don Aquilino. But in twisting his entire countenance toward our view, Kinski nevertheless offers the sight of his own eyes to both Don Aquilino and to us as stand-ins for the trapper's eyes and their claim to ecstatic truth. Kinski's gaze, in all its wide-eyed intensity and urgency, here wants to take on the same gravity and evidentiary force the French trapper in Fitzcarraldo's story demanded for his visual experience of Niagara Falls. His look was and is one breaking the frame of conventional definitions of truth and subjectivity. It not only collapses the divide between the near and the distant, but between image and reality, experience and world.

In turning toward the camera, Kinski draws Aquilino and us into what Western thought has come to call image as much as he lodges images in the vibrancy of his and our bodies. He not only dissolves stable borders between different ontological realities and planes of representation, but in so doing folds the performative and the authentic into one dynamic. There is no way for us to decide at this moment whether we see Fitzcarraldo or Kinski facing the camera; no way to determine whether his turn addresses diegetic or extra-diegetic onlookers; no way to ascertain whether Fitzcarraldo, in staring at the river, sees the passing waters of the Amazon or the raging rapids of the Ucayali before his inner eye; no way to settle whether Fitzcarraldo is mere medium or intentional agent. All we know is simply that Brian Sweeny Fitzcarraldo, as embodied by Klaus Kinski and as filmed by Werner Herzog, is a character much more complex than Romantic tropes of artistic genius, adventurous travel, and grandiose failure project. He takes risks and traverses dangerous grounds, not to feel the real more intensely, nor to embrace existential threats for their own sake, but first and foremost to explore the possibilities of a new ecology of images, to probe unorthodox metabolisms between viewer and viewed. What Fitzcarraldo's story has to do with the French trapper's is that it makes us contemplate concepts of seeing modeled on no less than the immersive, spherical, tactile, and resonant qualities of hearing—the way in which listeners live inside the world of sound rather than approach the audible as something physically detached from their own bodies.

"For me," Swedish auteur Ingmar Bergman once said in an interview with Roger Ebert, "the human face is the most important subject of the cinema."[27] As he turns to and offers his countenance to the eye of the camera, Kinski's face is much more than the screen of tormented individuality and self-expression to which Bergman was attracted. Kinski's face instead takes on the features of a landscape. It has a life of its own. This face is no mere outside to some mysterious inside, no mere surface expressing or encoding the complexities of an individual soul. Rather, what you see is what you get, and what you get is no longer anchored in traditional understandings of human subjectivity and self-contained individuality. Life flows across the landscape of Kinski's face like rivers stream through the jungle. To live dangerously is to live a life in which neither the borders nor the sovereignty of humanistic visions of the subject can or should be taken for granted anymore. It is to probe human perception as a resonance chamber of forces and intensities that exceed our control and desire. It is to explore different landscapes—rivers, rapids, trees, mountains, sounds, and faces—as mediums to stand outside ourselves, as grounds of the ecstatic.

In the Wake

In May 2018, three decades after the filming of *Fitzcarraldo*, Werner Herzog returned to Peru in order to conduct a ten-day master class for forty-eight aspiring filmmakers, with the promise that the best of their resulting work would be promoted for inclusion at future international film festivals. Although the location of the workshop, near the Tambopata National Reserve, one of the last virgin tropical rain forests in the world, had played no role in the making of *Aguirre* and *Fitzcarraldo*, the seminar's advertising—somewhat riddled with linguistic errors and stylistic infelicities—drew heavily on well-known tropes associated with Herzog's Amazon films in order to attract possible customers:

> After the first conquering adventure of Lope de Aguirre, Fitzcarraldo's obsession followed. And then, the obsession of Herzog himself who explored in *Burden of Dreams* the heavy weight his dreams meant. He would approach, as well, his conflicting relationship with the actor Klaus Kinski in *My intimate Enemy* [aka *My Best Enemy*, LK] and his evasion to death in *Wings of Hope*. The spiral of the jungle and time would later be closed with Brad Macallam's initiatory trip, the central character of *My son, my son, what have ye done*, that would become itself the representation of the beginning and the end of a madness created by the untameable nature. In his cinema and his savage prose, Werner Herzog reveals himself as a passionate pursuer of his vane dreams, a trait he shares with some of his most powerful characters. In May 2018 Werner Herzog will go back to the savage Peruvian landscapes, this time, to guide the creation of 48 young

> filmmakers who will come to live together, for the first time,
> the unique experience of making cinema imbedded of jungle
> and adventure.[28]

Though Herzog had offered various filmmaking seminars in challenging locations before, the 2018 master class was the first to be held in a natural setting that, in the eyes of many patrons of global art cinema, remain inextricably linked to Aguirre's, Fitzcarraldo's, and also Herzog's respective voyages into colonial darkness in the 1970s and early 1980s. In spite of the fact that the advertising campaign took various liberties with regard to both the proper allocation of authorship, the spelling of names, and the use of standard grammar, the appeal of "Filming in Peru with Werner Herzog" was tremendous and resulted in a speedy filling of the participant roster for this 5,000 Euro adventure. As indicated in the seminar ad and website, however, Herzog's 2018 return to the Amazon river basin was not his first after having concluded the filming of *Fitzcarraldo* in early November 1981. A made-for-TV documentary, *Wings of Hope* (1998) transported the viewer to the Peruvian jungle to reconstruct the harrowing experience of Juliane Koepcke, who in the early 1970s had survived an airplane crash after her plane had been struck by lightning. In asking Koepcke to recall and in fact re-enact her traumatic experience near locations that were central in the making of both *Aguirre* and *Fitzcarraldo*, Herzog with *Wings of Hope* clearly also sought to tap into and rework his own vexing past in the Peruvian jungle, including near-plane crashes and the experience of encountering (or in fact provoking) life-threatening situations amid the rain forest. The 1999 *My Best Fiend*, Herzog's documentary and essay film about his tension-ridden relationship with actor Klaus Kinski, included several sequences captured in Peru, most notably perhaps the one in which Herzog recalls the legendary opening shot of *Aguirre* near Machu Picchu and ruminates about the challenges of working with both unpredictable actors such as

Kinski and the contingencies of inhospitable landscapes. "While we were shooting," Herzog ponders, "I had a very profound feeling as if the grace of God was with this film and with me. As if I were witnessing something extraordinary which I would never see again. I can say, that on this day I definitely came to know my own destiny." And the 2009 American-German co-production *My Son, My Son, What Have Ye Done*, a sort-of horror film starring Michael Shannon, Willem Dafoe, and Chloë Sevigny, incorporated several scenes shot in the Amazon. The most memorable sequence is one in which Brad McCullam—the film's psychologically disturbed protagonist, hostage taker, and killer—in a flashback attempts to kayak down the Rio Urubamba, the very same river that served as a location for Fitzcarraldo's operatic failure and whose raging waters in this film are meant to explain the origins of McCullam's mental disturbance.

Herzog's nonfiction work has become known for its frequent scenes of choreographed re-enactment. Over and over again, we witness Herzog steering people who suffer from past trauma and violence back to the sites of their initial traumatization. The burden of painful pasts, in Herzog, is never something we can alleviate, let alone master, by means of cognitive reflection and self-reflexive strategies of "working through." Herzog's often seemingly perverse and cruel stress on re-enactment, on staging and recording uncomfortable returns of the past, instead suggests a different model of dealing with the imprints of painful events. We might call it homeopathic. It requires subjects to take in controlled doses of what originally afflicted their bodies and minds, to ingest a painful past into the present, so as to learn how to move beyond pain by learning how to move with it into the future.

It is tempting to understand Herzog's various returns to Peru and the Amazon basin after the shooting of *Fitzcarraldo* as homeopathic strategies of re-enactment as well: efforts to reconnect to a history of precarious filmmaking in order to adjust to carrying its weight. Critics and interviewers continue to press Herzog for a gesture of remorse about the danger and possible destruction the making of *Fitzcarraldo* may have caused. However, as proven in so many of his other films with subjects other than himself, Herzog's homeopathy of re-enactment leaves considerable space for much-needed atonement and regret. For Herzog, replaying past actions and experiences in a different key is a more appropriate strategy for dealing with challenging memories than is talking them through from the standpoint of detached reflection. Consider a critical scene in Herzog's 2004 *The White Diamond*, following aeronautical engineer Graham Dorrington to the rain forest in Guyana—six hundred miles north of Manaus and the Amazon River—and his efforts to fly a teardrop-shaped airship over the forest canopy near Kaieteur Falls. Throughout the film, Dorrington himself visibly suffers from Post-Traumatic Stress Disorder: one of his earlier expeditions caused the death of wildlife photographer Dieter Plage in the jungle of Sumatra. As Eric Ames has persuasively argued, Dorrington, with his dream of flying over the treetops, serves as a stand-in for Fitzcarraldo and his dream of bringing opera to the jungle.[29] But he also undoubtedly offers a double, an alter ego, for Herzog himself. In the sequence in question, Dorrington is about to launch his airship in spite of various concerns about its safety. Herzog enters the frame to intervene, yet not to convince the reckless pilot to abort his solo flight, but to convince him to take Herzog and his camera along for the ride. "There is such a things as follies," Herzog lectures Dorrington. "It would be stupid . . . to accept that you are flying without a camera on board." And he concludes memorably: "There are dignified stupidities, and there are heroic stupidities, and there is such a thing as stupid stupidities, and that would be a stupid stupidity not to have a camera on board. I am going to fly. I am going to fly with you." And so he does, much to the ensuing dismay of various technical crew members because the airship indeed runs into various troubles during its flight, yet without missing the point of Herzog's intervention, namely to gather impressive images whose

"Stupid Stupidities": *The White Diamond* (2004).

recording, according to Herzog, could not be entrusted to anyone but himself, due to the mission's danger.

In documenting Dorrington's efforts to levitate again without denying the burdens of the past, *The White Diamond* at the same time offers Herzog a platform to move on by at once recognizing and re-enacting some of the more precarious aspects of the making of *Fitzcarraldo*. The scene leaves little doubt that Fitzcarraldo's and Herzog's respective desires to haul ships over mountains lingers as a troubling memory—a burden that may strike individuals with the same kind of silence and stammering that Dorrington himself displays whenever he tries to recall his previous disaster in front of the camera. Though my reading of the scene may miss Herzog's intentions, his suggestion is to understand Dorrington's attempted solo aeronautical performance as a stupid stupidity, Fitzcarraldo's and Herzog's own nautical passage through the jungle as a heroic stupidity, and Herzog's present insistence not to allow danger and disaster to pass without capturing them on film as a form of dignified stupidity. Many viewers will not hesitate to consider all three of these distinctions as stupid altogether. What matters for our context, however, is that Herzog's intervention near Kaieteur Falls remains entirely true to his life-long politics and ethics of re-enactment: the homeopathic idea of replaying the past in order to reshuffle its weight, in order to relearn how to float by repeating history with a difference. No one, in Herzog's universe, speaks of victories over painful pasts, of conclusively coming to terms with the arresting impact of taxing memories. To endure, to learn how to move and take on different figurations of folly, is all and much more than most of us can hope for.

There are many good reasons to think that strategies of authorial re-enactment do not suffice to address the troubling recklessness of both the diegetic and extra-diegetic politics of *Fitzcarraldo*. Herzog himself is unlikely to serve as a direct interlocutor in such conversations. His more explicit statements about the legacy of

Fitzcarraldo over the last four decades often sound like those records Kinski seeks to play to his invisible audiences in the film: sound bites frozen in time, repeating thoughts and phrases as if history had not moved since 1982. If we want to look elsewhere to explore other approaches, two more recent exemplary efforts come to mind: the 2015 multi-channel video installation *Halka/Haiti 18°48'05"N 72°23'01"W* by Polish artists C. T. Jasper and Joanna Malinowska, and the 2018 novel *Stromland* (River Land) by German writer Florian Wacker. These two works do not simply think through what in retrospect appears precarious about *Fitzcarraldo* and its making, but actively question Herzog's politics of re-enactment and *Fitzcarraldo*'s staging of cultural encounters in the jungle.

Curated by Magdalena Moskalewicz, *Halka/Haiti* premiered at the Venice Biennale in 2015 as Poland's official contribution to this much-noted mega-exhibition of contemporary art. The 82-minute film, cast by four projectors onto a curved screen to provide a near-360 degree immersive viewing experience, documented a performance of Stanisław Moniuszko's nineteenth-century opera *Halka* in the small village of Cazale in Haiti, a town partly inhabited by descendants of Polish soldiers who in a rather unlikely turn of history fought on the side of Haitian revolutionaries against their French colonial oppressors around 1800. The town's winding main dirt road serves as an open space for the performance. Singers in heavy costume enter the visible field from unexpected locations; brought from Port-au-Prince, the orchestra is perched under a tree and inside an unfinished construction site on the right; spectators flock together in various groups dispersed across the entire square and screen; a goat—tied to an electricity pole—takes up a prominent position in the left foreground, but shows no signs of being affected by the commotion; clattering motorcycles traverse performance and screen repeatedly. Similar to Fitzcarraldo's dream of bringing Italian opera to the jungle, *Halka/Haiti* at once stages and documents a rather improbable encounter between nineteenth-century European high art and Europe's former colonies. And like the curious ending of *Fitzcarraldo*, Jasper and Malinowska emancipate opera from the separate confines of established institutions of art in order to release its aesthetic energies into the topographies of the everyday. And yet, whatever we see (and hear) during the film is inspired not simply to revisit, but explicitly to reframe and correct the Romantic exoticism and imperial aestheticism of the single-minded effort of Herzog's protagonist Fitzcarraldo to collapse cultural differences into homogenous spectacles of aesthetic ecstasy.

First staged in 1854, *Halka* tells a tragic love story between the Polish peasant girl Halka and the nobleman Janusz. The latter will eventually abandon his lover in order to marry the socially more appropriate Zofia, whereas Halka in a dramatic final scene throws herself into a river, unable to endure the shame and disappointment her cross-class affair has cast upon her. The opera's central themes—unfulfilled love and suicide caused by rigid class divisions—were certainly staples of eighteenth- and nineteenth-century European stage art. In spite of the fact that the opera's music did not include any folk elements and its libretto did not recount mythic stories of origin, *Halka* nevertheless came to emerge as Poland's national opera of sorts, in part because its tale of abusive power and desperate sacrifice helped trigger unifying affects within a national culture haunted by forced divisions and repeated reorientations.

As curious as it may at first appear to stage this opera in an open-air setting in rural Haiti, it is as perplexing to see Polish actors in elaborate costume while Haitian musicians provide the orchestra music for their singing and local audiences, with various levels of attention, behold the action in their midst. The film starts in the morning hours of the day of the performance and then follows the actual spectacle in one continuous take, captured by multiple cameras and projected across the curved screen in what amounts to a captivating horizontal panorama. This immense and uncut spread of things visible (and audible) invites the audience not to enter a state

Top: Polish Pavilion at the 56th International Art Exhibition – La Biennale di Venezia. Photo by Barbara Kaja Kaniewska. Courtesy of Zachęta–National Gallery of Art. Bottom: C. T. Jasper & Joanna Malinowska in collaboration with Magdalena Moskalewicz, *Halka/Haiti 18°48'05"N 72°23'01"W*, 2015. Still from a multichannel video projection. Photo by Barbara Kaja Kaniewska, Mateusz Golis. Courtesy of the artists and Zachęta–National Gallery of Art.

of affective absorption, as one at first might assume, but quite the opposite: to peruse the visual field without ever seeing the whole, to actively focus on different and shifting zones of action, to isolate details independently, to follow the paths of spectators across the screen, to stay alert to the fact that nothing that can be seen in *Halka/Haiti* aspires to fuse and be fused into one seamless representation of cultural homogeneity. To see *Halka/Haiti* is to enter a zone in which spectatorial immersion and investigating detachment go hand in hand. It is to experience the curious presence of Polish opera in the tropics as a laboratory to probe our own perception, the push and pull between the horizontal screen's ability to immerse ourselves in the action and the image's structural refusal to offer us a monarch-of-all-I-survey perspective, that is, the master trope of imperial and neocolonial vision as celebrated in the shot of Kinski taking in the sight of trees discussed at the beginning of this book.

Artist and co-director Joanna Malinowska, when asked about *Fitzcarraldo*'s Romantic rhetoric of quest and failure, remarked: "A character's lonely failure to reach either spiritual or geographical heights shapes and defines Romantic dramaturgy. *Fitzcarraldo*, although shot and written in a relatively recent past, and set in early-twentieth-century Peru, is a perfect representation of this nineteenth-century ideal. But as with most narratives that end with a spectacular fiasco, one always wonders how it could have ended differently. Our project reverses the predetermined fortune of a Romantic hero—a product of the period that roughly coincides with the revolution in Haiti, times of Napoleon, and the creation of *Halka*."[30] Rather than wanting to provide compelling images and sounds, *Halka/Haiti* set out to ask a series of open-ended questions: What really happens when you bring European opera to the "jungle"? What does it take to empower productive collaborations across boundaries and cultural differences? How can filmmakers work in challenging locations without—like Herzog—romanticizing inhospitable landscapes as topographies of the mind and soul? What is at the center of this film's aspiration to reverse *Fitzcarraldo*, however, is no less than the effort to debunk operative myths of radical cultural specificity and alterity, and in so doing, to undercut the exoticizing rhetoric of the sublime that drives both Fitzcarraldo's and Herzog's encounters with forbidding landscapes and non-Western populations. In *Halka/ Haiti*, the people of Cazale and the Polish singers and crew members may meet each other like kindred spirits: both are products of long histories of colonial domination, both in fact can look back to shared ancestors several centuries ago. And yet, *Halka/Haiti* does everything at its disposal to represent this encounter between Western high art and today's Global South in all its heterogeneity and unevenness: as something that cannot be but experimental, ephemeral, performative, and aware of its own strangeness and unlikeliness; as something that does not force anyone to become and be other, but instead uses the legacy of nineteenth-century European opera as a platform to probe the possibilities and limits of cultural exchange and collaboration in a postcolonial, albeit by no means harmonious, present.

Florian Wacker's novel *Stromland*, published in March 2018, adds intriguing dimensions to how contemporary artists such as Jasper and Malinowska seek to reframe and reverse *Fitzcarraldo*, the film's narrative as much as the history of its making. Mostly set in 1984, the novel tells the story of Irina and her boyfriend Hilmar traveling to Peru from West Germany in search of Irina's twin brother Thomas, who after having served as a member of the film crew of *Fitzcarraldo* disappeared, seemingly without any trace, in the Amazon jungle. While the novel, in its use of place names and geographical features, leaves it unclear whether we are moving through real existing territories or the kind of fictionalized landscapes Herzog fabricated for *Fitzcarraldo*, the path marked for the reader carries us deep into a world in which the real and the cinematic increasingly blur into each other, the hallucinatory presses on and displaces the tangible, and afterimages of Aguirre's final madness come to dominate over Fitzcarraldo's reckless yet clearly goal-oriented folly. As will become clear, Thomas's at once exhilarating and frustrating work for Herzog and with Kinski motivated him to remain in Peru to experiment with various drugs in the hopes of accessing the spiritual depth of arboreal landscapes, the animated and animating power of the Amazon forest. Though Irina in the end will fail to find her twin brother in the jungle, she instead discovers a seemingly utopian community of German immigrants, the Wilhelmi clan. During a drug-induced ceremony, their leader Richard sleeps with her and—as we are to learn later—fathers a child meant to be the future heir of the community's land. Meanwhile, we learn that the German immigrants' utopian existence isn't as utopian as it appears: various family members supply Pablo Escobar's Columbian drug operations with cocaine fabricated in hidden labs on the estate. The novel's final pages carry us from the early 1980s to present-day Frankfurt, staging a first-time encounter between Richard and his adult daughter Katja. Thomas is still believed to be somewhere in Peru. Katja's mother now lives in Hamburg, her once promising career path permanently derailed by her Amazon experience. The novel ends with Katja learning that she will eventually inherit an estate of about sixty soccer fields in size in Peru, causing her to toy with the idea of traveling there; and with Richard traveling north to Hamburg in the hope of reconnecting with Irina.

Thomas's involvement in the making of *Fitzcarraldo* looms large over the entire narrative setup of *Stromland*. His experience as assistant to cinematographer Thomas Mauch—we are to learn—was challenging and disenchanting. As he writes in one of his letters to his "little" twin sister:

> Fuck the movie, fuck Klaus and Werner! I do prefer Klaus, though. He is a madman, screams, always wants to be the center of attention, but I can handle that. He gets his coffee, he gets approval, he can yell at the forest. Werner is much worse. I understand him only gradually, and what I understand, it scares me, little sister. For him, there is only

the film, only the material, nothing else. I think he hates the jungle and the birds, in all this he only sees death, rotting. He does not understand that it is a cycle, over and over again. The gentle beeping of young birds arises from the screams, the forest draws new strength from the dead body of a monkey. It's not about life and dying, because if it were, it would be a terrible slaughter. He does everything to make this film a reality. He is obsessed with it. He gives the Indians money, buys their loyalty, he has the forest cleared, they toil like slaves. I will go to Pucallpa and from there by plane back to Iquitos. My skin itches. Art requires sacrifices, it is said, all great directors are obsessed, but at what price? For a popcorn-eating audience that, as soon as it leaves the cinema, has already forgotten the images?[31]

Stromland is a novel of uncanny entanglements, ironic reversals, and ominous misunderstandings and repetitions. Irina enters the lands of the making of *Fitzcarraldo* only to face a world that resonates much more with Aguirre's imperial dreams, his mad vision to conquer lands and found dynasties the like of which the earth has never seen. In search of the real that remains after making a film, Irina experiences the Wilhelmi estate as nothing but grand theater, a spectacle in the forest true to Fitzcarraldo's aspirations: "All this was just a big show, an opera production among the trees; the men and women wore costumes and moved according to set rules, and at the end of each day they left the scenes and returned to the surrounding villages" (309). And instead of finding her lost brother, Irina—as the novel's ending suggests—herself gets lost, unable to live up to the promise her life as a young adult projected.

Stromland's perhaps most illuminating commentary on *Fitzcarraldo* lies elsewhere, namely in exploring the biting proposition that Germans, when seeking to go primitive in the jungle, when embracing the rain forest's inhospitability as a ground on which to play out existential quests and crises, search for and find little more than themselves. In their geographical forays into the lands along the real or fictionalized Rio Ucayali, neither Thomas and Irina, nor—by implication— Fitzcarraldo and Herzog ever encounter more than just projections of their own making. Though their respective actions clearly impact the lives and ecologies of indigenous people, they remain much closer to home than they presume. The Amazon is sublimely foreign only because it is stacked with the familiar: with literal and metaphorical specters of Western fantasies and, as it turns out, German efforts to transport things German to the jungle. That *Stromland* ends somewhere between Frankfurt and Hamburg, and not in the thickets of the rain forest, is only consequential. What is wrong with neo- and postcolonial settlers, explorers, desperados, junkies, happiness seekers, operatic entrepreneurs, and filmmakers in the jungle is the fact that they on some level never left home in the first place.

According to Herzog, *Fitzcarraldo* commenced with a compelling mental image:

> A vision had seized hold of me, like the demented fury of a hound that has sunk its teeth into the leg of a deer carcass and is shaking and tugging at the downed game so frantically that the hunter gives up trying to calm him. It was the vision of a large steamship scaling a hill under its own steam, working its way up a steep slope in the jungle, while above this natural landscape, which shatters the weak and the strong with equal ferocity, soars the voice of Caruso, silencing all the pain and all the voices of the primeval forest and drowning out all birdsong. To be more precise: bird cries, for in this setting, left unfinished and abandoned by God in wrath, the birds do not sing; they shriek in pain, and confused trees tangle with one another like battling Titans, from horizon to horizon, in a steaming creation still being formed. Fog-panting and exhausted they stand in this unreal misery—and I, like a stanza in a poem written in an unknown foreign tongue, am shaken to the core.[32]

"A vision had seized hold of me."

As they, more than three decades after the making of *Fitzcarraldo*, reframe the putative attractions of opera in the jungle, neither *Halka/Haiti* nor *Stromland* articulate much patience with Herzog's rhetoric of sublime shudder. Jasper and Malinowska's multi-channel video installation probes the extent to which Western music can soar in the tropics without silencing the sounds of local populations and romanticizing the other and unknown as a site awaiting Western protagonists to complete its unfinished existence. Wacker's novel reveals that Herzog's and Fitzcarraldo's shudder about the foreign is much more about the self, the known but forgotten and repressed, than about the complexities of life in the jungle: the presumed misery of the rain forest is nothing but a projection of Herzog's own misery, and the difference between dignified, heroic, and stupid stupidities is no more than a self-righteous illusion. No matter whether viewers and readers sign on to the physical and cultural challenges Herzog embraced when going to the Amazon, what Jasper and Malinowska and Wacker indicate is a profound need to address and work through the impact *Fitzcarraldo* continues to have on our imagination, our understanding of the politics of film and authorship, our thinking about the power of art, our maps of colonial and postcolonial encounters.

Herzog's efforts to stage spectacles in the Amazon remain deeply provocative and ambiguous. They pose too many unresolved questions to relegate *Fitzcarraldo* to a closed chapter of film history. There is no end in sight of us hauling Herzog's film over the messy mountains of time, no river in view that could promise the end of this film's contested course through history. Similar to Sisyphus in Albert Camus's famous reading,[33] we do well to recognize our perennial struggle with *Fitzcarraldo* not simply as a form of punishment, but as an opportunity to reflect on the conditions and limits of happiness.

CREDITS

Director:
Werner Herzog

Writer:
Werner Herzog

Production Companies:
Werner Herzog Filmproduktion
Project Filmproduktion
Filmverlag der Autoren
Zweites Deutsches Fernsehen (ZDF)
Wildlife Films Peru

Produced by:
Werner Herzog (producer)
Renzo Rossellini (associate producer)
Walter Saxer (executive producer)
Willi Segler (producer)
Lucki Stipetic (producer)

Cast:
Klaus Kinski (Brian Sweeney Fitzgerald,
    aka Fitzcarraldo)
Claudia Cardinale (Molly)
José Lewgoy (Don Aquilino)
Miguel Ángel Fuentes (Cholo)
Paul Hittscher (Captain, aka Orinoco Paul)
Huerequeque Enrique Bohorquez
    (Huerequeque, the cook)
Grande Otelo (Station master)
Peter Berling (Opera Manager)
David Pérez Espinosa (Chief of Campa
    Indians)

Music:
Popol Vuh

Cinematography:
Thomas Mauch

Film Editing:
Beate Mainka-Jellinghaus

Production Design:
Ulrich Bergfelder
Henning von Gierke

Costume Design:
Gisela Storch

Runtime:
158 min

Sound Mix:
Mono

Color:
Color

Aspect Ratio:
1.85 : 1

Camera:
Arriflex 35 BL3

Film Length:
4,322 m

Negative Format:
35 mm

Cinematographic Process:
Spherical

Printed Film Format:
35 mm

Production Costs:
DM 14 Million (inflation adjusted ca.
    $17–23 Million in 2018)

Release Dates:
March 1982 (West Germany), May 1982
    (France), October 1982 (USA)

NOTES

1   Werner Herzog, *Conquest of the Useless: Reflections from the Making of "Fitzcarraldo,"* trans. Krishna Winston (New York: Ecco, 2009), 140.

2   Herzog, *Conquest of the Useless*, 294–95.

3   J. R. McNeill and Peter Engelke, *The Great Acceleration: An Environmental History of the Anthropocene* (Cambridge, MA: Harvard University Press, 2014).

4   Christophe Bonneuil and Jean-Baptiste Fressoz, *The Shock of the Anthropocene: The Earth, History and Us* (New York: Verso Books, 2016) Kindle edition, locations 577–83.

5   Clive Hamilton, *Defiant Earth: The Fate of Humans in the Anthropocene* (Cambridge, UK: Polity Press, 2017) Kindle edition, locations 200–201.

6   Mary Louise Pratt, *Imperial Eyes: Travel Writing and Transculturation* (New York: Routledge, 1992), 205.

7   David Grann, *The Lost City of Z* (New York: Random House, 2009), 87.

8   Georg Friedrich Wilhelm Hegel, *The Philosophy of History*, with prefaces by Charles Hegel and the translator J. Sibree (Kitchener, Ontario: Batoche Books, 2001), 44.

9   For an eye-opening reading of this scene, see Richard John Ascárate, "Have You Ever Seen a Shrunken Head?' The Early Modern Roots of Ecstatic Truth in Werner Herzog's *Fitzcarraldo,*" *PMLA* 122, no. 2 (2007): 483–501.

10   Mihaly Csikszentmihalyi, *Flow: The Psychology of Optimal Experience* (1990; New York: Harper Perennial, 2008).

11   Csikszentmihalyi, *Flow*, 71.

12   Veronica Strang, *Water: Nature and Culture* (Islington, UK: Reaktion Books, 2015), 33.

13   Arthur Schopenhauer, *The World as Will and Representation*, trans E. F. J. Payne (New York: Dover, 1969), I, 264.

14   For a more detailed reading of this sequence and a discussion of the overall role of opera in Herzog's work, see Lutz Koepnick, "Archetypes of Emotion: Werner Herzog and Opera," in *A Companion to Werner Herzog*, ed. Brad Prager (Chichester, UK: Wiley-Blackwell, 2012), 149–67.

15   John Durham Peters, *The Marvelous Clouds: Toward a Philosophy of Elemental Media* (Chicago: University of Chicago Press, 2015), Kindle edition.

16   For a detailed and engaging reading of the use of gramophone technology in *Fitzcarraldo*, see Richard Leppert, *Aesthetic Technologies of Modernity, Subjectivity, and Nature: Opera, Orchestra, Phonograph, Film* (Berkeley: University of California Press, 2015), 56–73.

17   Salomé Voegelin, *Listening to Noise and Silence: Toward a Philosophy of Sound Art* (New York: Continuum, 2010), xii.

18   Christoph Cox, "Beyond Representation and Signification: Toward a Sonic Materialism," *Journal of Visual Culture* 10, no. 2 (2011): 153.

19   Many thanks to the press's anonymous reviewer of this manuscript for pointing out to me the scale model's history. Built by Henning von Gierke at the Bavaria Film studio in Munich, the model ship experienced a curious journey and afterlife of its own. For a while it served as a decoration for a discotheque in northern Germany before it finally came to rest as part of the collection of the Deutsche Kinemathek/Museum für Film und Fernsehen in Berlin: https://www.deutsche-kinemathek.de/sites/deutsche-kinemathek.de/files/public/node-attachments/pm_mollyaida.pdf.

20   *Herzog on Herzog*, ed. Paul Cronin (New York: Faber and Faber, 2002), 176.

21   Kristen Whissel, *Spectacular Digital Effects: CGI and Contemporary Cinema* (Durham, NC: Duke University Press, 2014).

22   Whissel, *Spectacular Digital Effects*, 6.

23   Tom Gunning, "The Cinema of Attractions: Early Film, its Spectator and the Avant-Garde," in *Early Cinema: Space, Frame, Narrative*, ed. Thomas Elsaesser and Adam Barker (London: BFI Publishing, 1990), 56–62; and Tom Gunning, "An Aesthetic of Astonishment: Early Film and the (In)credulous Spectator," in *Viewing Positions: Ways of Seeing Film*, ed. Linda Williams (New Brunswick, NJ: Rutgers University Press, 1995), 114–33.

24   André Bazin, "Cinema and Exploration," in *What is Cinema?*, trans. Hugh Gray, vol. 1 (Berkeley: University of California Press, 1967), 161.

25   Ernst Jünger, "Photography and the 'Second Consciousness': An Excerpt from 'On Pain,'" trans. Joel Agee, *Photography in the Modern Era: European Documents and Critical Writings, 1913–1940*, ed. Christopher Phillips (New York: Metropolitan Museum of Art / Aperture, 1989), 208.

26   Reprinted in Eric Ames, *Ferocious Reality: Documentary according to Werner Herzog* (Minneapolis: University of Minnesota Press, 2012), ix.

27   https://www.rogerebert.com/interviews/ingmar-bergman-in-memory.

28   http://www.blackfactorycinema.com/taller2018/?lang=en.

29   Eric Ames, "The Case of Herzog: Re-Opened," in *A Companion to Werner Herzog*, ed. Brad Prager (Chichester, UK: Wiley-Blackwell, 2012), 405–6.

30   Magdalena Moskalewicz, *Halka/Haiti 18°48'05"N 72°23'01"W by C. T. Jasper and Joanna Malinowska* (New York: Inventory Press, 2015), 137.

31   Florian Wacker, *Stromland: Roman* (Berlin: Berlin Verlag, 2018), 135–36.

32   Herzog, *Conquest of the Useless*, 1.

33   Albert Camus, *The Myth of Sisyphus and Other Essays*, trans. Justin O'Brien (New York: Vintage International, 1991), 1–138. "I leave Sisyphus at the foot of the mountain. One always finds one's burden again. But Sisyphus teaches the higher fidelity that negates the gods and raises rocks. He too concludes that all is well. This universe henceforth without

a master seems to him neither sterile nor futile. Each atom of that stone, each mineral flake of that night-filled mountain, in itself, forms a world. The struggle itself toward the heights is enough to fill a man's heart. One must imagine Sisyphus happy." (123)